Volunteers of America® & SCHOLASTIC

And Thornhill Learning Center

Present this book to:

_____

_____

There are no limits to caring.®

www.VolunteersofAmerica.org
1-800-899-0089

AUTOIMMUNE DISEASES

AUTOIMMUNE DISEASES

Nathan Aaseng

A Venture Book
Franklin Watts
New York Chicago London Toronto Sydney

Photographs copyright ©: Photo Researchers, Inc.: pp. 17
(David M. Phillips), 29 (Michael P. Gadomski), 44 (Larry Mulvehill/SS),
53 (SPL); The Bettmann Archive: pp. 19, 50; John Kappler/Philippa Marrack:
p. 32; National Library of Medicine, Prints and Photographs Collection:
p. 40; WHO Photo: p. 51; Custom Medical Stock Photo/NMSB: p. 56;
National Multiple Sclerosis Society: p. 59; UPI/Bettmann: pp. 61, 92;
UN Photo: p. 62; The Office of George Bush, Houston, TX: p. 82;
Lynn Adams: p. 87; Reuters/Bettmann: p. 95.

Library of Congress Cataloging-in-Publication Data

Aaseng, Nathan.
Autoimmune diseases / Nathan Aaseng.
p. cm. — (A Venture book.)
Includes bibliographical references and index.
ISBN 0-531-12553-X (lib. bdg.)
1. Autoimmune diseases—Juvenile literature. [1. Autoimmune diseases.
2. Immunologic diseases. 3. Diseases. 4. Immune system.] I. Title
RC600.A27   1995
616.97'8 — dc20   94-49443
                                          CIP AC

CONTENTS

AUTOIMMUNE DISEASES

1
AUTOIMMUNE ATTACK

At first, my four-year-old son Evan seemed to be battling a typical winter illness. He felt miserable, had no energy, and looked a little pale. He had a bit of a fever and "sick breath," which indicated some sort of cold or upper respiratory infection. For three nights he kept my wife and me awake with a relentless cough.

On Saturday, Evan began falling asleep at the snap of a finger. He would be talking or playing, and after turning away from him for only a couple of seconds, we would find him sound asleep at some odd angle on the couch. "Poor kid," we thought, as he napped for the fifth time that day. "Being up coughing all night has really wiped him out."

The next day Evan seemed a little better. But as he walked out of the bathroom, he remarked, with only a trace of surprise in his voice, "My potty is brown."

We knew he was referring to his urine, and my wife and I became concerned. But because he did not seem upset, we were puzzled as to what he meant. Was the urine just a little darker than usual, not worth bothering about? Or was there blood in the urine—a sure sign that he should see a doctor?

We asked him to call us the next time he had to go to the bathroom. Later that afternoon he did, and we were horrified to see urine the color of burgundy wine. Something was seriously wrong. We rushed Evan to the clinic, where the doctor took one look at his urine sample and directed us to the local hospital.

The emergency room personnel performed a few tests and then recommended that Evan be taken to a better equipped children's hospital at the University of Minnesota. He appeared to have some kind of kidney malfunction. After being given only half an hour to pack, we took off on a ninety-mile ambulance ride through the winter night. By this time Evan's skin was as white as the snow that blew across the road, while the whites of his eyes were yellow.

The doctors at the hospital quickly recognized that the problem was not with Evan's kidneys. But they were not certain just what was going on. We looked on helplessly as Evan's red blood cell count dropped so low that the medical staff became concerned. Evan continued to fall asleep suddenly and frequently, and he remained a pasty white. The lack of red blood cells was probably putting a great strain on his heart. We could do nothing more than pray and hope that Evan's immune system would correct itself before it was too late.

The technicians drew blood frequently to measure what was happening in Evan's system. We stayed with Evan through the night and waited anxiously for each new report. Finally, the blood tests showed that Evan had a disease called autoimmune hemolytic anemia. *Autoimmune* meant that something had gone wrong with Evan's immune system. Instead of attacking only foreign invaders, it was attacking his own tissues.

Anemia meant that he had a shortage of oxygen-carrying red cells in his blood. *Hemolytic* meant that something was destroying those red blood cells.

Simply put, Evan's immune system had mistaken red blood cells for germs and was killing them as fast as possible. In contrast to acquired immune deficiency syndrome (AIDS), in which the immune system can barely function at all, this disease caused his immune system to go into overdrive.

Unfortunately, the medical experts could do little for Evan. Their primary weapons against his condition could not be deployed in his case. They had drugs that could shut down the immune system and thereby slow or stop the destruction of cells. But Evan also had a mild respiratory infection. If the immune system were turned off, that infection could rage unchecked throughout his body.

The doctors could try giving him a blood transfusion to replace the red blood cells he had lost. But Evan's immune system would surely attack the transfused blood cells as furiously as it did Evan's cells. All that could be done was to flush a salt solution through his system by an intravenous tube to prevent his kidneys from being damaged.

About twenty-four hours after we had checked into the hospital, the blood cell count stopped dropping. The next blood sample showed the count again remaining stable, and we dared hope his system was getting back under control. The following reading dropped slightly, raising anxieties again. But by the middle of the second day in the hospital, we were all breathing a sigh of relief as Evan's condition stabilized. Whatever glitch had caused his immune system to go haywire apparently had been shut off.

Evan recovered quickly. By the end of the third day in the hospital, he was feeling and looking more like his old self. His condition had improved so dramatically that he was allowed to go home. The best news of all was that the physicians did not expect any further problems. Chances were good that Evan would not have any recurrence of the autoimmune disease. Evan was very lucky; it is unusual for patients with this disease to recover naturally, without being given medication to suppress the immune system.

WHAT IS AUTOIMMUNE?

The term *autoimmune disease* has been used for many years in the medical community to describe any condition in which the immune system mistakenly attacks its own body's healthy tissues (*auto* means "self"). The term is not well known among the general public, but that is likely to change soon. Recently, to the surprise of the medical community, researchers have been finding that many common diseases are caused by an autoimmune attack. Medical experts now classify more than forty diseases of the human body as either definitely or probably autoimmune diseases. Some are fairly widespread illnesses such as rheumatoid arthritis, multiple sclerosis, and the most serious form of diabetes.

Taken all together, autoimmune diseases affect a significant number of people—roughly 5 to 7 percent of the population. They are a major cause of severe disabilities and long-term recurring pain and fatigue.

Evan's hemolytic anemia is not one of the more common autoimmune diseases. But two elements of his illness are common to most autoimmune diseases. First, almost all autoimmune diseases appear without warning or apparent cause. Even the lingering, life-long autoimmune diseases—rheumatoid arthritis, for example—tend to go in cycles of flaring up and fading away for no apparent reason. Second, most autoimmune patients suffer from fatigue as a result of the body's battle with itself.

Evan's disease, however, is not a typical example of an autoimmune disease, simply because there is no such thing as typical in autoimmune diseases. An overzealous immune system can cause a wide variety of conditions, depending on which part of the body it attacks. It can strike with life-threatening ferocity, or it can develop slowly and painfully, causing such minor discomfort that a person never bothers to seek treatment. Many autoimmune diseases last a lifetime; some appear briefly and then go away forever. Some can be easily controlled, while others are extremely difficult to treat.

Autoimmune diseases are more consistent in the people they strike than in the symptoms they produce. For example, they are far more likely to attack women than men. And they tend to appear most often during or shortly after puberty. People in their forties and fifties also get them in high numbers, though not as high as in teenagers. But as Evan's case indicates, autoimmune diseases are not restricted to any age or sex.

2

THE IMMUNE SYSTEM: THE BODY'S DEFENDER

Autoimmune diseases have baffled medical experts for centuries, mainly because until recently very little was known about the immune system. Without a thorough understanding of how the immune system functions, there was no way of understanding how it might malfunction.

The field of immunology began in the late nineteenth century when scientists such as Louis Pasteur of France and Robert Koch of Germany proved that human diseases could be caused by microscopic bacteria. Researchers discovered that the human body is an ideal home for a great number of tiny creatures—not only bacteria, but protozoans and viruses as well. When any of these almost invisible creatures penetrates the skin or enters through air passages, it finds a warm, moist environment filled with readily available nutrients.

Early medical researchers found that some of these invaders reproduce so rapidly that if they are not somehow stopped, they can quickly take over the body, causing sickness or death. However, they also saw many people recovering from an attack by these rapidly producing, deadly organisms. Why? What stopped the tiny creatures from overwhelming these people?

In 1888 the Russian microbiologist Elie Metchnikoff provided the first evidence that the body could actively defend itself against these microscopic invaders. While looking at blood under a microscope, Metchnikoff saw for the first time large, colorless cells. Unlike the red blood cells, which carry oxygen throughout the body, the white cells seemed much like tiny animals that wandered through the bloodstream, eating bacteria and other impurities in the blood. Metchnikoff named these cells, *phagocytes*, which means "cells that eat."

The discovery of phagocytes showed that the body had a built-in defense system for fighting off disease agents. But this system proved to be far more complicated than first supposed. One complication was chemicals in the immune system called *antitoxins*. Scientists working at about the time of Metchnikoff's discovery found that the deadly disease diphtheria was caused by a poison, or toxin, produced by a bacteria. The German biologist Emil von Behring then studied the blood of the fortunate people who survived diphtheria. He found that their blood contained a chemical capable of neutralizing the diphtheria toxin, so he called the chemical an antitoxin.

Even more intriguing, Behring found that only people who had contracted diphtheria had this antitoxin in their blood. Thus, he concluded the substance must be manufactured by the body specifically to fight against the diphtheria toxin. Researchers soon discovered other chemicals that work in the immune system in similar ways. Some of them could neutralize toxins, while others appeared to destroy bacteria. All of them were most noticeable immediately after an infection.

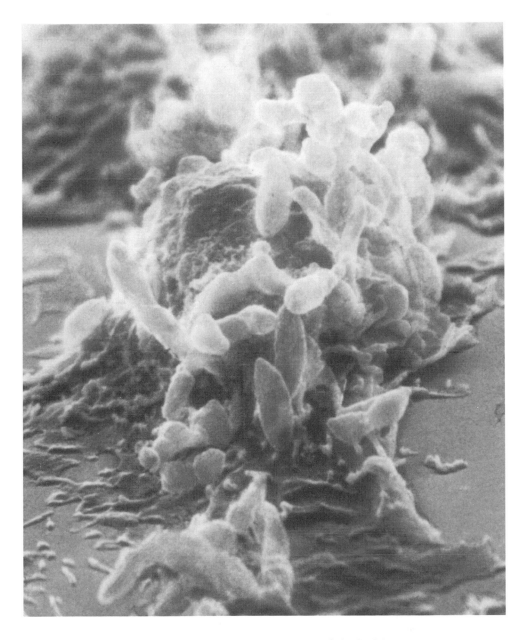

White blood cells are an important part of the body's immune system. Here a white blood cell is eating rod-shaped bacteria.

Since some of the chemicals do not target toxins, they were given the general name *antibodies*. Antitoxins then became a subgroup within antibodies. In the 1930s, researchers discovered that antibodies consist of protein molecules with unusual shapes. In fact, the molecules on the surface of the protein seemed to be a mirror image of the molecules on the surface of the invading, disease-causing bacteria or toxins. Eventually researchers concluded that antibodies search for their targets by trying to match their surfaces with molecules passing by. Known as *surface markers*, the molecules on the surface of cells and other entities act as ID cards, broadcasting their identity to others. When antibody and intruder fit together like a lock and key, the antibody binds to its enemy.

The presence of the antibody on its surface prevents the disease organism from doing any harm. But the main role of the antibodies seems to be to "mark" invading organisms so that the phagocytes can easily find and devour them. In 1948 researchers isolated the group of white blood cells that manufacture these antibodies. Eventually the antibody-making cells became known as *B-lymphocytes*, or *B-cells* for short, because they are made in bone marrow. *Lymphocytes* are a type of white blood cell with a large nucleus and are distinct from phagocytes.

Another type of lymphocyte, the *T-cell*, was discovered in the 1960s. This immune cell was named for the *thymus*, a gland near the neck that produces T-cells. T-cells turned out to be the "sentries" who roam throughout the body, hunting for harmful bacteria, viruses, protozoans, toxins, or other particles. These harmful entities are collectively known as *antigens* because they cause the immune system to *gen*erate *anti*bodies.

The T-cells travel through the bloodstream, but they can also wriggle through the spaces between cells

18

*German biologist Emil von Behring discovered that
the immune system produces antitoxins to fight
specific poisons in the body. In the photo, he is injecting
a guinea pig with tetanus germs so that it will
produce tetanus antitoxin.*

all over the body. They challenge every entity they
meet—every piece of dust or virus or molecule of protein. First they identify whether it is a legitimate part
of the body or an unauthorized invader by examining
its surface markers. If the entity turns out to be an ac-
ceptable part of the body, the T-cell leaves it alone and
continues its scouting mission. But if it is recognized
as foreign, the T-cell sounds the alarm: it activates the
immune system, which in turn produces antibodies
and sends phagocytes to the infected area.

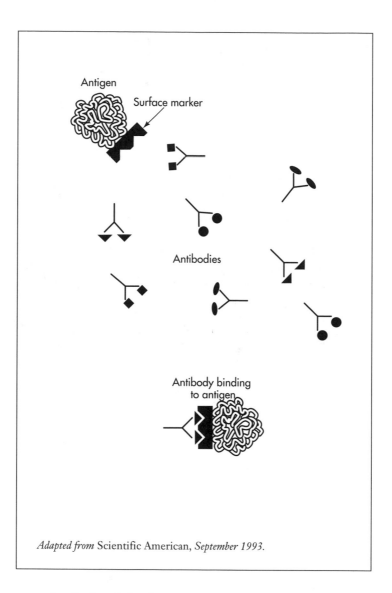

Adapted from Scientific American, *September 1993.*

*Antibodies fight disease organisms called antigens.
Each antibody is designed to attack an antigen
displaying a specific surface marker. If they fit together
like pieces of a puzzle, the antibody locks on and
the antigen becomes harmless.*

Just how the T-cell could distinguish between a harmful antigen and a valuable part of the body remained a mystery for many years. Nor did anyone know how the different chemicals in the immune system could coordinate their attack against invaders with such precision.

In recent years, though, scientists have been closing in on the fascinating secrets of the body's defense against disease.

THE MARVELS OF THE IMMUNE SYSTEM

Scientists have discovered that the immune system is a marvelously complex defense network that involves one of every hundred body cells, roughly one trillion total cells. This enormous arsenal of cells is controlled by a vast communications network that has two key features:

- A memory system that cells can call upon to distinguish harmful invaders from necessary body molecules
- A specific response to ensure that the antigens are destroyed with minimal damage to innocent bystander cells

Scientists are not certain how the body makes up its original list of what is foreign and what is "self." The logical time to take inventory would be before birth, when a baby is shielded from external environmental antigens. Indeed, scientists believe that white blood cells circulate through the fetus before birth and catalogue the body's molecules. Then, after birth, all molecules encountered by immune cells as they patrol the body are matched against this original list.

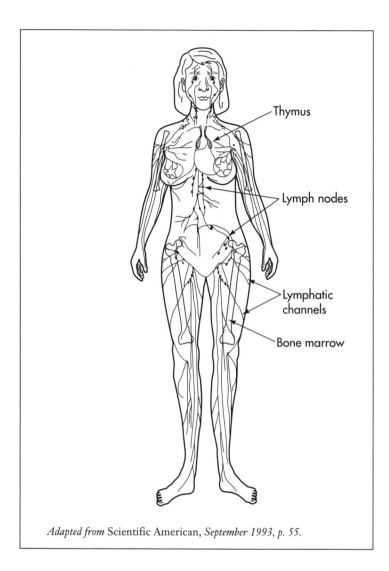

Thymus

Lymph nodes

Lymphatic channels

Bone marrow

Adapted from Scientific American, *September 1993, p. 55.*

The immune system is a complex defense network consisting of lymphatic channels that spread throughout the body like blood vessels. Immune activity such as antibody generation takes place in the lymph nodes. B-cells are born in bone marrow, and T-cells come from the thymus.

The immune system cells display intricate teamwork in identifying and attacking foreign invaders. Some B-cells break off a piece of the invader and display it on their outer surface. These cells, known as antigen-presenting cells (APCs), do not judge whether a molecule is harmful or not; they merely present the evidence. A T-cell on patrol intercepts the APC and reads its surface marker to determine whether it is an enemy or friend. If an enemy, the T-cell will call the entire immune system into action.

Most T-cells can recognize only one particular antigen. The human body contains millions of different T-cell types, each on the lookout for a particular enemy. The T-cell recognizes its assigned enemy by fitting the fragment held up by the APC into a receptor on the T-cell surface. In the same way an antibody matches an antigen, the receptor has a shape that matches the antigen fragment. It acts much like the ignition on a car: it can be turned on only with a particular key. The vast majority of surface fragments that the T-cell tests will not fit into the receptor. When that happens, the T-cell moves on to challenge another fragment held up by another APC.

But if the fragment does fit, the T-cell knows it has encountered an enemy. Sparked by the T-cell, the entire immune system roars to life. Through dozens of chemical reactions, the T-cells summon the immune system firepower needed to defeat the invasion. Some of the T-cells, known as killer T-cells, can directly destroy the antigen.

Other T-cells stimulate a local inflammation reaction at the infection site. Tiny blood vessels swell so that large antigen-eating phagocytes can more easily enter the area. And to make the environment more uncomfortable for the invader, the tissues begin to produce fluid and body heat increases.

Still other T-cells leave the site and enter *lymph channels*, a specialized network of passageways through which agents of the immune system travel over the body. These cells carry with them a pattern of the antigen's surface markers as they search for the B-cells that can manufacture the one antibody that is effective against that particular invader. The T-cells, called *T helper cells*, chemically activate the proper B-cells so that they become antibody factories, churning out vast amounts of the needed antibody.

The antibody factories are located in *lymph nodes*, small lumps of tissue distributed throughout the lymph network. Here, the T-cells also begin reproducing rapidly so that more T-cells are available to turn on more B-cells. Within a short amount of time, the immune system is spewing out a veritable flood of antibodies that swarm over the infection site. There, the antibodies attach themselves to the surface markers of the invading antigens.

As mentioned before, the antibodies not only flag the antigen as enemy, they prevent the antigen from causing further damage. They also make the infecting agents clump together into large targets that the phagocytes and other killer immune cells can then easily destroy. Immune cells that have been invaded and damaged add more firepower to the attack by releasing chemicals that attract greater numbers of cell eaters to the infected area.

When the invader has been defeated, the antibodies, the swelling, and other immune reactions are no longer needed. In fact, if they continue they can make a person most uncomfortable. T-cells have the final task of emitting chemicals that shut down the immune reaction once the danger of infection is over.

But the immune system response does not completely disband after an infection. Instead, it forms a preventive line of defense in case the antigen strikes

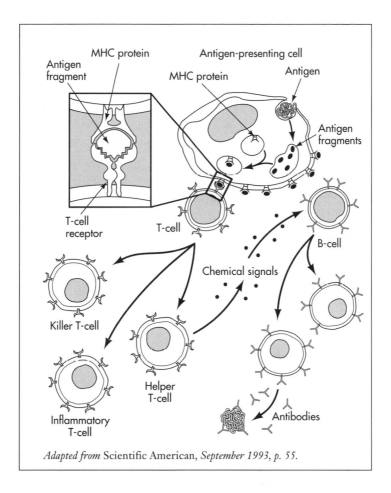

Adapted from Scientific American, *September 1993, p. 55.*

The immune system goes into action when a T-cell responds to a B-cell known as an antigen-presenting cell. The antigen-presenting cell breaks off a piece of the antigen, combines it with a protein called MHC, and displays them on its surface for inspection by the T-cell. When the T-cell recognizes an enemy, it begins fighting the infection in several ways. Killer T-cells try to destroy it directly; inflammatory T-cells cause the infection area to become inflamed; and helper T-cells chemically activate the appropriate B-cells so that they begin reproducing and making antibodies.

again. Without this defense, rapidly reproducing bacteria and viruses could overwhelm the sparse immune system defenses in the initial stages of an infection. A person may be ill for days or even longer before the immune system overcomes the invaders' head start and manufactures enough weaponry to defeat them. There is always the risk that the immune system could lose the battle during this period.

So once the immune system has suffered damage from an antigen, it is especially alert for another attack by that antigen. The B-cells continue to manufacture some antibodies that neutralize the antigen so that the next time the invader penetrates the body, the immune system is ready for it. The existing antibodies may be able to stop the infection before it gets started. When this happens, a person is said to be immune to the illness.

The immune system is usually highly effective in warding off disease. The lock-and-key method ensures that the immune system targets only the invading antigen; the antibodies do not attack cells they are not supposed to attack. Furthermore, the body quickly builds up a huge supply of just the right antibodies to fight the disease without wasting time and energy manufacturing unneeded antibodies. Finally, the immune system shuts down most of its attack to protect the body from unwanted side effects, but adds a line of defense as insurance against antigens that have proved harmful.

The body's immune system, however, is neither foolproof nor invincible. In the never-ending attempt to gain access to the human environment, bacteria and especially viruses have evolved elaborate strategies for defeating or bypassing the immune system. Over the course of a few generations they may alter the shape of their surface receptors. This means that the flu virus that attacks today may be quite different from an ancestor virus that attacked the same person years ago. The change may be significant enough that the antibodies built up against the virus years ago no longer work, and so the person has no immunity to the virus.

Immune systems vary from person to person. Some people have such effective immune systems that they are able to fight off the most widespread diseases. While cold and flu epidemics sweep their community, they never get sick. Others seem to catch whatever "bug" is going around. Their immune systems are less efficient in fighting off infection. As we grow older, we tend to become immune to more illnesses as our immune system gains experience with different antigens. Older people, for example, get far fewer colds than do small children.

On the other hand, our immune systems tend to wear out or break down as we get older. That makes us more susceptible to illnesses such as cancer.

WHAT CAN GO WRONG WITH THE IMMUNE SYSTEM

As marvelously sophisticated as the human immune system is, it occasionally does more harm than good. The most obvious problem arises when harmless foreign particles and organisms enter the body. Many immune systems cannot easily distinguish between foreign molecules that cause damage and those that do not. As a result, they sometimes attack a harmless substance, causing uncomfortable symptoms in the process.

If the immune system attacked every foreign particle that entered the body, we could not survive. Food, for example, contains many molecules that the immune system identifies as being foreign. Yet these molecules are necessary to maintain life. What does the immune system do with these suspect invaders? In most cases, it learns to make an exception for the foreign particles that pass through the intestine.

But sometimes, certain foods are misidentified as enemy invaders. This can provoke an immune response so severe that body tissues swell and other symptoms of illness appear. The person is said to be allergic to that food and must avoid eating it.

There are many different kinds of allergies. Pollen is another example of a harmless substance that triggers an immune response. The watering eyes and runny nose of hay fever are the result of the immune system's launching an attack on what it has falsely labeled a dangerous enemy. Allergy sufferers would be far better off if their immune system could learn to leave the pollen alone.

A more dangerous kind of allergic reaction is called *anaphylactic shock*. It results from a violent immune system reaction to a normally harmless substance, such as shellfish, or a mildly harmful substance, such as bee venom. The massive swelling caused by the immune response may restrict or stop breathing or restrict blood flow. The condition can be fatal.

Another instance in which the immune system causes medical problems is during transplant procedures. The immune system identifies the cells of a transplanted organ such as a kidney or heart as foreign. The same goes for transplanted tissue such as skin and bone. For many years transplants proved difficult because the body's immune system relentlessly attacked the foreign cells.

Surgeons have found two ways to get around the problem of rejection. First, they carefully match transplant recipients with donors so that their cells are as genetically similar as possible. Relatives of the recipient are ideal donors because they share many of the

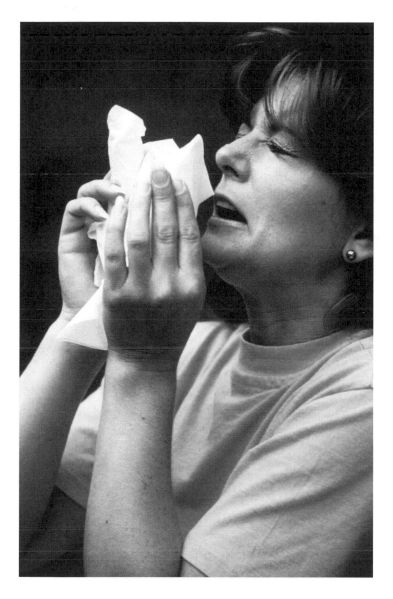

*When people have allergies, the immune system
mistakenly attacks a harmless substance such as pollen.
Sneezing, runny nose, and itchy eyes are the result of
this misguided immune response.*

same genes. Second, they administer drugs that suppress the patient's immune system so that it does not attack the transplanted tissue.

As much trouble and suffering as these immune reactions cause, autoimmune diseases are much more serious, if only because they are inexplicable. For some reason, the immune system wrongly targets healthy body tissue as a foreign invader and directs an attack against it.

What would cause the immune system to make such a disastrous mistake and attack the body it is supposed to protect? Many immunologists believe that autoimmune diseases occur when something goes wrong with the T-cells. An attack on the wrong enemy is, after all, a matter of missed communication, and the T-cells are responsible for much of the communication within the immune system.

One explanation might be that the T-cells are somehow tricked by viruses or bacteria into attacking the wrong cells. Perhaps the surface markers of the enemy antigens closely resemble those of "self" molecules. The immune system might then produce antibodies that would attack the body tissue identified as the antigen. This type of response is known as a *cross-reaction*.

Scientists have applied the principle of cross-reactivity to create vaccines. By injecting a person with a relatively harmless organism that is similar to a harmful one, doctors can provide immunity to deadly diseases. The antibodies that the body produces against the harmless organism are ready to react against the harmful one, should it ever invade the body.

Another possible explanation for autoimmune diseases involves T-cells that cannot distinguish self cells from foreign cells. Some immunologists have proposed that the immune system occasionally produces these renegade T-cells accidentally and that they are normally kept under control by some self-policing immune mechanism. But if something goes wrong with the mechanism, the renegade cells may proliferate in numbers large enough to wreak havoc.

The unruly T-cells may get so out of control that the control mechanism finally kicks in, reacting quickly and harshly to shut them down. This would explain why so many autoimmune diseases erupt spontaneously and then fade away without any apparent reason. In this reasoning, everything remains quiet until the renegade cells again tip the balance.

As a matter of fact, Phillipa Marrack and John Kappler, a husband-and-wife immune-research team working in Denver, Colorado, have found evidence of a regulating mechanism. They discovered that many of the T-cells forming in the thymus did not recognize the difference between self molecules and foreign molecules.

Marrack and Kappler identified and studied one type of T-cell as it formed in the thymus glands of mice. They found that some of the cells showed signs of attacking the mice tissue. Few of these renegade cells, however, escaped the thymus alive. The body apparently has some sort of regulating mechanism that eliminates dangerous, self-attacking cells.

Marrack concluded that we do have immune cells that react to our own body, but we purge most of them before they are mature so they can't damage us.[1] If this is the case, then autoimmune diseases may be caused by a failure of the regulating mechanism.

Marrack believes that a few of these autoimmune T-cells regularly escape from the thymus. But in most cases they are too few or too weak to cause any real

Researchers John Kappler and Philippa Marrack are working to find out why the immune system attacks its own body's tissues in autoimmune diseases.

problem. Nearly everyone, for example, has T-cells in his or her blood that will react against nerve tissue. Yet fewer than one person in one thousand develops an autoimmune disease against this tissue. Marrack believes that autoimmune diseases may occur when something "turns on" these normally insignificant cells.

Other researchers suggest that the problem may not be with the T-cells but with the immune system mechanism that teaches T-cells to recognize the self molecules. A group of genes, known as major histo-compatibility complex (MHC), hold the key to the body's identification of self molecules. The genes instruct cells to make MHC proteins, which become surface markers on cells. In essence, these surface markers are "free passes," permitting the cells to remain in the body with no danger of attack from the immune system. When B-cells (specifically, APCs) display an antigen on their surface for examination by T-cells, they combine it with an MHC protein, as if offering a comparison between an authentic molecule and a suspicious intruder.

Diane Faustman of the Harvard Medical School has conducted experiments showing that the amount of MHC proteins is significantly diminished in human diabetics. If these MHC proteins are absent or not working correctly, the T-cells may never learn to identify properly the molecules they challenge. In that case, they could easily mistake body tissues for foreign antigens.

Genetics plays a role in the immune system breakdown that results in autoimmune diseases, though no one is certain exactly what that role is. Rheumatoid arthritis and systemic lupus erythematosus (see Chapter 3), for example, appear to run in families. Identical twins, who share the same genes, are more likely to have the diseases than are fraternal twins, who have only some genes in common. Rheumatoid arthritis has been found to develop in a greater percentage of people with a specific gene than of people without the gene. Furthermore, researchers have found several *genetic markers*, or segments of genes, that, when present in a person's DNA (deoxyribonucleic acid), indicate a greater-than-normal susceptibility to type I diabetes. All these facts point toward an inherited genetic cause of immune system malfunctioning.

On the other hand, the genetic aspect of autoimmune diseases so far has created more questions than answers. Many people who have autoimmune diseases have no history of the disease in their family. And only a small minority of people who have genes associated with autoimmune diseases ever get the disease. These facts indicate that defective genes are only part of a chain of cause and effect.

Immune system experts do not speak of genes as causes of autoimmune disease. Rather, they regard genetic factors as making a person more or less vulnerable to immune system problems. Most believe something else is responsible for setting autoimmune diseases in motion. The question that has really baffled researchers is: What might that something else be?

AUTOIMMUNE TRIGGERS

Although immunologists have made great strides in understanding the workings of the body's defense system, they are nowhere near finding the "smoking gun," the evidence of what triggers the immune system to attack the body it is designed to protect.

The most likely culprits are bacteria and viruses. Autoimmune diseases frequently appear in people who have recently been ill with some kind of infection. Evan's hemolytic anemia, for example, came on the heels of a sinus infection and respiratory illness. Children with rheumatoid arthritis often show signs of bacterial or viral infection just before the disease appears. The Swiss immunologist R. M. Zinkernagle believes that many diseases thought to be autoimmune are probably linked to as yet unknown viruses.

Phillipa Marrack has developed a scenario that would explain how bacteria and viruses might be able to trigger autoimmune diseases. She suggests that certain antigens called *superantigens* may be capable of confusing the immune system. A normal antigen fits only into the T-cell receptor designed to recognize it. But a superantigen acts much like a master key; it can open up many T-cell receptors. As a result, the immune system recognizes that a harmful invader is present but is so confused by the antigen's surface marker that it cannot figure out exactly what the invader is. Instead of counteracting the superantigen by producing one specific antibody that works against it, the immune system unleashes a wild, blind barrage of immune activity in hopes that something will knock out the invader.

This type of response is known to happen with certain bacteria such as the staphylococci that cause food poisoning. These bacteria give off a toxin that triggers a response in many different types of T-cells. All these T-cells fire off chemical messages to their various B-cell counterparts as well as to other immune system components. The result is a poisonous overdose of immune activity that makes the person extremely ill.

A superantigen may stimulate thousands of different types of T-cells. Immunologists including Marrack suggest that an autoimmune disease might be caused when a chaotic, hyperactive immune reaction to a superantigen happens to overstimulate some of the normally ineffective, self-attacking T-cells. These T-cells send messages to B-cells, causing them to crank out an army of self-attacking antibodies, or *autoantibodies*. The autoantibodies then spread out through the body looking for the "enemies" that they are supposed to attack. The enemy, of course, is a specific type of its own tissue. Autoantibodies that attack joints produce arthritis, those that attack blood cells produce hemolytic anemia, and so on.

In 1991 Marrack and Kappler demonstrated that superantigens can be produced by viruses as well as bacteria. Bacterial and viral infections have been closely linked with some autoimmune diseases, especially one called Guillain-Barré syndrome. In the fall of 1991, German and American researchers found that *Yersinia enterocolitica*, a bacteria that causes infection of the digestive tract, can initiate a thyroid disease in rats similar to another autoimmune disease called Graves' disease.

While these are intriguing bits of evidence, no definite connection has yet been found between infections and most autoimmune diseases. That may be because the infections trigger a delayed autoimmune reaction, long after the bacteria or virus has left the scene. Or it could be that the medications taken to combat autoimmune illnesses eliminate any bacteria or virus that might be present. Or there may be something other than bacteria or viruses that triggers autoimmune diseases.

Some scientists point to the increased incidence of autoimmune diseases in modern times as evidence that buildup of poisons or pollutants in the environment may be an autoimmune trigger. Trichloroethylene (TCE), an industrial cleaner common in spot removers and paint strippers, has been singled out as a possible trigger. Tests have shown that low-level exposure to the chemical over a long period may be connected with autoimmune diseases. However, no clear-cut cause-and-effect relationship has been found. Lithium, a chemical used in batteries and psychiatric drugs, has been implicated in diseases of the thyroid gland.

Professor Gian Franco Bottazo Hazo of London, however, points out that the recent rise in autoimmune diseases can be explained by factors other than pollution. For example, an autoimmune virus could have coexisted harmlessly with humans for many years and then suddenly became dangerous.

Leakage of silicone from breast implants is also suspected of triggering autoimmune diseases. The UCLA rheumatologist Steven Weiner has seen autoimmune diseases develop in more than five hundred women with breast implants. He argues that in at least 125 of those cases, the disease is clearly connected to the implants. He points out that more than half of the patients improved when the implants were removed.

Implant manufacturers contend that these connections are only coincidence and point to a thirty-year safety record. Nonetheless, the Food and Drug Administration has asked for a voluntary halt to breast implantation.

Other possible triggers being investigated include stress, health habits, and diet. Stress has been shown to cause changes in the immune system. Prolonged stress can intensify symptoms of autoimmune disease such as fatigue, pain, and nervousness and has been connected with arthritis flare-ups.

Proper sleep, exercise, and nutrition all help the immune system do its job effectively. Vitamins, for example, have recently shown some promise as disease-preventing agents. And studies have demonstrated that the symptoms of rheumatoid arthritis improve when patients fast or eat low-fat, low-protein, low-calorie diets. Experiments also show that the use of alcohol and tobacco can hinder the immune system.

None of these negative health factors, however, has actually been shown to trigger an autoimmune disease. There are only two things that can be said with confidence about why autoimmune diseases strike certain individuals at a certain time:

- They tend to develop in individuals who are susceptible as a result of genetic inheritance or an unhealthy lifestyle
- They may be triggered by something in the environment, whether it is bacteria, viruses, superantigens, toxins, pollutants, or tissue damage

The greatest challenge facing autoimmune researchers is tracking down the elusive evidence that will pin down once and for all what triggers the immune system to begin attacking itself.

WHAT ARE THE AUTOIMMUNE DISEASES?

This chapter highlights some of the more common of the forty known or suspected autoimmune diseases. It also offers a representative sampling of less common self-attacking diseases.

RHEUMATOID ARTHRITIS

Arthritis and rheumatism, or something with very similar symptoms, have been afflicting people since the dawn of history. Descriptions of stiff, painful joints—the hallmark of arthritis—were recorded in Egyptian writings dating as far back as six thousand years ago. World conquerors such as Alexander the Great and Julius Caesar complained of arthritic symptoms. Rheumatism, which is an inflammation of bone and surrounding tissue, encompasses arthritis, as well as conditions involving bone other than joints. The word *rheumatism* comes from the term the ancient Greeks gave the condition—*rheumaticos*.

Nearly forty million Americans, roughly one out of every six people, suffer from some form of arthritis.

*Arthritis afflicted world conqueror Alexander the Great,
who lived in the fourth century B.C. This artwork shows
him in bed being examined by his physician Philippos.*

The broad category of arthritis includes more than
one hundred different diseases that affect the joints.
Some of the diseases are categorized as autoimmune
and some are not.

Rheumatoid arthritis, one of the more serious and
painful forms of arthritis, is an autoimmune disease.
Its painful symptoms are caused by an immune system
attack on the bones, ligaments, tendons, and cartilage
in and around joints. Most experts agree that this ill-

ness has become widespread in the world only since the nineteenth century. Yet it is the most common of the autoimmune diseases, afflicting 2.5 million Americans—one out of every hundred.

Despite its prevalence, research on arthritis has lagged behind studies of less common conditions that, for one reason or another, attract more attention. Most observers believe arthritis has been put on the back burner because it is not regarded as life-threatening. It is generally viewed as simply a nuisance. Many people have the impression that arthritis is just a natural process of aging in which the joints get a little stiff and bent.

But anyone who has experienced rheumatoid arthritis knows it is not trivial, nor is it just a natural consequence of getting old. Even though the disease does not directly cause death, it can be a dangerous, even devastating, illness. Studies have shown that the diminishing quality of life impacts rheumatoid arthritis sufferers so deeply that it reduces their life expectancy by at least three and as much as eighteen years. The pain and frustration of arthritis also take their toll on personal relationships, causing a divorce rate significantly higher than that of the general population.

A minority of rheumatoid arthritis sufferers, just under 20 percent, become so crippled that within ten years of being diagnosed with the illness, they are unable to use their hands or to walk. According to one arthritis expert, "Probably no other disease results in so much suffering in so many people for such a long period of time" as rheumatoid arthritis.[1] Americans spend over $12.7 billion a year treating the disease, primarily to relieve the frequent, excruciating pain. As much as $1 billion is wasted on fad cures.

As in many autoimmune diseases, rheumatoid arthritis strikes females more often than males—

nearly three times as often. The illness is most likely to develop between the ages of twenty and forty, but it can occur at any age. Rheumatoid arthritis is not contagious. There appears to be a specific gene, known as DR4, connected with rheumatoid arthritis: those who have the gene are more likely to get the disease. Yet only a small minority of those with DR4 ever have rheumatoid arthritis. Researchers have not been able to discover exactly what triggers the disease in susceptible individuals.

Symptoms of rheumatoid arthritis usually appear in the smaller joints. More than 70 percent of cases predominantly affect the hands and feet. The disease may first appear as a stiffness in the hands upon rising in the morning. Pain and swelling in the joints increase as the disease progresses. Unlike other types of arthritis that cause problems in only one or two joints, rheumatoid arthritis often attacks many joints. It can also affect organs, such as the eyes, heart, lungs, skin, muscle, and nerves.

The discomfort of rheumatoid arthritis often makes sleep difficult. As one patient describes it, "A night of this pain can seem like two years."[2] Lost sleep, together with the fatigue of fighting off constant pain, can leave arthritis sufferers exhausted much of the time. In addition to specific pain, people with the disease often feel generally sick, with a dull ache that feels almost like having the flu.

Like many autoimmune diseases, rheumatoid arthritis varies greatly in severity. Some cases inflict only moderate discomfort. Other cases destroy joints and connective tissue, gradually crippling the patient. Arthritis sufferers have good days when the disease goes into remission; in other words, the symptoms go away. Remission can last for days or weeks or even longer.

Arthritis patients also have bad days when the joints suddenly flare up and the pain is nearly unbearable. This, too, can last for a variable amount of time. Remissions and flare-ups occur without warning and without any apparent cause. Such conditions as humidity or a change in the weather can bring about flare-ups.

Diagnosis of the disease is sometimes tricky. A doctor might suspect rheumatoid arthritis after merely hearing a patient's symptoms. Often, however, doctors mistakenly diagnose depression because of the constant fatigue the patient experiences. A physical examination of the patient usually reveals the redness and joint inflammation commonly associated with rheumatoid arthritis. Skin nodules are sometimes also present. If an entire set of joints is inflamed, rheumatoid arthritis is more likely to be the cause than other kinds of arthritis.

While a physical exam may indicate rheumatoid arthritis, doctors will usually order laboratory tests to confirm the diagnosis and to get a better understanding of how the disease affects the particular patient. A blood test can reveal the presence of an autoantibody connected with the disease. The test is not foolproof, however, since the autoantibody is present in only 75 to 80 percent of patients with the disease. That's because the autoantibody seldom appears during the early stage of rheumatoid arthritis. The amount of fluid in the joints can also reveal the extent of rheumatoid arthritis, since the fluid builds as the disease progresses.

When they suspect rheumatoid arthritis, doctors often take X rays of bones to see whether they show any nodules, thinning or weakening, or excessive wear. However, X rays cannot detect the soft structures of the body, including tendons, ligaments, and cartilage.

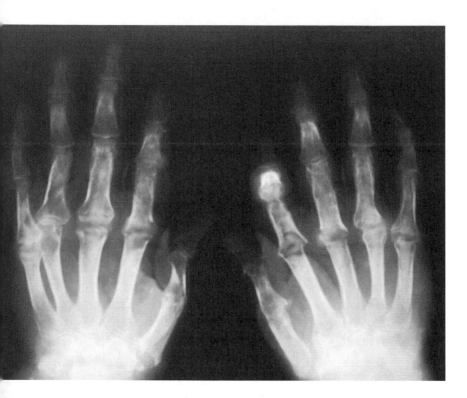

*An X ray shows evidence of arthritis in the
right index-finger bone.*

To determine whether these tissues have been affected
by the disease, physicians may call for magnetic resonance imaging (MRI), which creates a computer-gen-
erated, three-dimensional image of soft body tissues
by applying magnetic waves to the body.

Because arthritis ailments come and go so mysteri-
ously, miraculous claims of home remedies and fad
cures are common. A person whose arthritis goes into
remission at the time he or she begins to take Chinese
herbs or bee venom will likely believe that the remedy

44

has been marvelously effective. It's no surprise then that arthritis remedies are a billion-dollar business.

The truth is that there is presently no cure for rheumatoid arthritis. Accepted medical treatments are designed to relieve the symptoms of pain and swelling, and to prevent or retard the destruction of joint tissue. The over-the-counter pain reliever aspirin has been the primary medication for arthritis ever since it became commercially available in 1899. Because it must be taken in very high doses, however, it can cause stomach problems in many people.

After the isolation in the 1930s of *cortisone*, a steroid produced by the adrenal glands, it was for a time touted as a miracle drug in the treatment of arthritis because it reduced swelling and relieved pain. Unfortunately, repeated doses of cortisone produced many side effects, including skin disorders, heart problems, susceptibility to infection, insanity, liver problems, brittle bones, and stomach ulcers. As a result, cortisone treatments quickly diminished.

Gold compounds, which reduce inflammation and suppress the immune system, have also been tried for many years. But they produce harsh side effects in as many as a third of the patients who take them.

Gold compounds and other drugs also lose effectiveness over time. Recently, a drug called methotrexate has become a popular treatment for arthritis because it can control symptoms in a large proportion of arthritics for five years or longer. Like other drugs, methotrexate has side effects, but they seem to be serious only when there are other complications, such as liver disease, kidney disease, lung problems, or heart failure.

Patients can take a number of steps on their own to improve their condition. Both cold and heat can relieve some arthritic symptoms. Mild heat can reduce pain and loosen joints. Ice packs on the joints can relieve pain and reduce swelling. Patients can alternately apply cold and heat, or they may find that one works better than another. Neither heat nor cold should be applied for more than fifteen to twenty minutes at a time.

Arthritis sufferers should change positions frequently to keep joints limber. This is especially important for people who sit at a desk all day. Patients should also modify their activities so they do not put too much stress on affected joints. Yet one of the worst things that someone with rheumatoid arthritis can do is avoid using the joints completely. Rheumatoid arthritis sufferers need to keep active to prevent their joints from deteriorating.

Stretching, swimming, walking, isometrics, and mild aerobics are good exercises for staying limber. These activities should be carefully monitored and cut back if they cause lingering pain. If patients must take pain relievers such as aspirin or cortisone to do an exercise, that activity should be stopped.

Stress reduction, proper diet, and rest are also important in helping a person cope with the discomfort of rheumatoid arthritis. Medical experts now say that with proper health care and medication, the vast majority of people with rheumatoid arthritis can go to work, get a full night's sleep, excercise, and even participate in sports.

TYPE I DIABETES

Only recently has the medical world linked the most serious form of diabetes, known as type I, to autoimmune diseases. It has long been known that the illness is caused by the lack of a natural hormone called *insulin*. But in 1988 researchers discovered that the blood of patients with type I diabetes contains antibodies against the pancreas cells that produce insulin. That evidence strongly suggested the disease is caused by an immune system attack on those cells.

About 700,000 Americans have type I diabetes. Also known as juvenile or insulin-dependent diabetes, the disease usually begins in early adolescence—most frequently between the ages of ten and twelve in girls and between twelve and fourteen in boys. Victims must have insulin injections to stave off symptoms of the disease. In contrast, type II diabetes, which accounts for 95 percent of diabetes cases, usually strikes after the age of forty. Although people with this form of diabetes are also relatively insulin-deficient, their symptoms can be managed through modifications in diet along with oral medicines and exercise. Type II diabetes has shown no signs of being an autoimmune disease.

Type I diabetes was one of the earliest diseases to be documented by historians. Records more than thirty-five hundred years old describe an ailment called "honey urine." In the ancient Middle East, there were reports of a disease called "Persian fire," in which victims complained of constant thirst. The name *diabetes* was coined by the Greek physician Arteus nearly eighteen hundred years ago.

But the mysteries of this disease have been slow in unraveling. Not until 1700 did an English doctor, Matthew Dobson, demonstrate that a diabetic's blood was abnormally high in sugar. For centuries after his finding, no one knew what caused the condition nor how to treat it. The disease typically raged uncontrolled, and the body wasted away. Victims often went into coma; death was inevitable.

Near the turn of the twentieth century, researchers finally discovered why people with diabetes have so much sugar in their blood. Their bodies are unable to use blood sugar, or *glucose*, as other people's bodies do. Glucose is a simple sugar produced by the breakdown of carbohydrates in food; it travels through the bloodstream to supply cells with fuel. The cells of nondiabetics convert the glucose to energy for the building and maintenance of the cells. But the cells of diabetics are unable to take up the glucose from the blood. Consequently, these cells are forced to consume the only sources of energy available to them— the fat and muscle of their own bodies. That explains the rapid weight loss that accompanies type I diabetes.

Meanwhile, the unused sugar stays in the bloodstream and causes other problems. It builds up to such high levels that the kidneys, whose job is to remove waste from the blood, have trouble dealing with it. The body's desperate efforts to eliminate the sugar result in symptoms of constant thirst and frequent urination. Another complication of high levels of sugar in the blood is long-term damage to the walls of large blood vessels.

Although physicians at the turn of the century understood much of what was happening in diabetics, they still did not know why the blood sugar was not being taken up by the body cells. In 1899 the German scientists Oskar Minkowski and Joseph von Mering removed the pancreas from a dog and found that diabetes developed in the animal. That was the first clue that the pancreas was somehow involved in the disease. Repeated attempts to discover the nature of the connection failed until 1920.

Then a young Canadian doctor named Frederick Banting began some experiments with the help of Charles Best, a biochemist. The two men ground up the pancreases of two dogs and extracted a small amount of fluid. They injected the fluid into a dog who was nearly dead of diabetes. The dog immediately woke up from a coma and appeared relatively healthy. The researchers measured the dog's blood sugar level and found that it had dropped.

Banting's and Best's experiments proved that this pancreatic fluid, which was eventually named insulin, was the key to blood sugar processing. Insulin turned out to be a hormone that unlocks the cells of the body so that glucose can enter and fuel them. Most people have insulin. People with diabetes do not. The discovery, and the synthetic manufacture of insulin, have since saved the lives of many diabetics.

Still, the experiments left an important question unanswered. Why are people with diabetes unable to produce insulin? The answer did not come until 1988, when researchers discovered that the immune system was attacking insulin-producing cells in the pancreas. That is when they began classifying type I diabetes as an autoimmune disease.

Before scientists completely understand type I diabetes, one remaining layer of mystery must be solved: what causes the immune system to attack the insulin-making cells? If genetic factors play a part, that role is difficult to sort out. White people have the disease in higher numbers than other races, and people in the Scandinavian countries have the highest incidence of type I diabetes in the world. The disease is not inherited as eye color is, but *susceptibility* to it runs in families. Brothers and sisters of type I diabetics are twenty times more likely to have the disease than people with no diabetic siblings. But many cases occur in families with no history of diabetes.

A person's susceptibility to a disease shows up in genetic markers. A genetic marker is a piece of genetic coding (DNA) that appears frequently in people with a certain characteristic or condition. About one in four people with diabetes carries at least one genetic

*Charles Best and Frederick Banting discovered that
insulin could keep people with diabetes relatively healthy.
They are shown here with the first diabetic dog
they kept alive with insulin.*

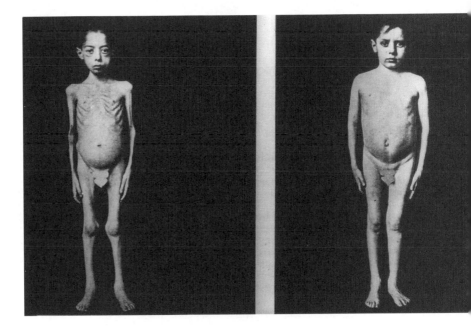

The photo on the left shows a child wasting away from diabetes before Banting and Best treated him with insulin in 1922. The same child is shown on the right only two months later.

marker linked with type I diabetes. Researchers have discovered, for example, an abnormal MHC gene in both human diabetics and diabetic laboratory mice. Recall from Chapter 2 that the protein produced by the MHC gene is combined with the antigen when B-cells present it to the T-cells for inspection.

Also, about 80 percent of those who have type I diabetes have an antibody to a protein produced by the insulin-making cells of the pancreas. This could indicate that the genetic fault in MHC causes the protein to be incorrectly presented to the T-cell scouts, who mistakenly identify them as enemies. Yet this explanation still does not account for why only a small percentage of individuals with genetic factors marking them as susceptible ever have the disease.

A recent study by Finnish and Canadian researchers at the Hospital for Sick Children in Toronto has uncovered evidence that early exposure to cow's milk may sometimes trigger type I diabetes. Breast-fed babies in the studies were less likely than milk-fed babies to have diabetes. Also, laboratory rats with genetic markers for diabetes remained free of the disease when milk was withheld from their diet.

Researchers traced the trigger to a particular protein in cow's milk. Normally the immune system tolerates foreign proteins that enter through the digestive tract. But the scientists believe that fragments of the cow's milk protein provoke a misguided response that destroys pancreas cells.

Other researchers suspect that a virus triggers the autoimmune reaction in diabetes.

At present, there is no cure for type I diabetes. Since Banting's and Best's discovery, insulin injections have been the primary treatment. Insulin cannot be taken orally because the digestive system would break it down before it could do any good. Most diabetics give themselves one or two injections of insulin per day. These shots generally combine a quick-acting insulin that is effective for four to six hours with a slower-acting form that works throughout the day.

A decade-long study completed in 1993 by the National Institutes of Health (NIH) found that more frequent shots may help people with diabetes live longer and stay healthier. The study, conducted at twenty-nine United States and Canadian medical centers, found that the blood sugar level of diabetics can fluctuate dramatically within a matter of hours. The

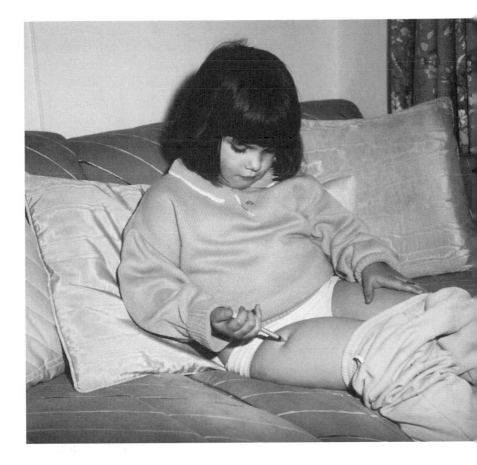

A five-year-old gives herself an injection of insulin.

high blood sugar levels that may occur between shots can lead to severe health problems over time—particularly with the eyes, heart, and kidneys. Diabetes is the leading cause of new blindness and kidney failure in Americans under the age of sixty-five. The NIH study showed that the risk of these complications can be cut by up to 75 percent with more careful monitoring and control of the blood glucose.

The study advised patients to check their blood sugar level as often as six to twelve times a day. The ability to monitor blood glucose with inexpensive meters makes this practical. The diabetic pricks his or her finger and places a drop of blood on a specially treated strip of paper. This paper slides into the glucose meter, which displays the blood sugar level within a minute or two. In response to the readings, patients following the guidelines give themselves more frequent insulin injections to keep blood sugar consistently down. The main danger with such stepped-up treatment is that the blood sugar levels might become too low. Low blood-sugar levels cause impaired thinking, unconsciousness, and even seizures. A careful balance between food intake and insulin injections is essential.

Diet is important for people with diabetes. Basically, it is the same healthy diet recommended for almost everyone. They must limit sweets because the simple sugars in them cause a rapid rise in blood sugar level. Also, to keep their system in balance, they must not skip meals.

Many people with diabetes were formerly advised to avoid strenuous exercise, particularly contact sports. But researchers have found that exercise makes insulin more efficient in helping cells take up glucose. Furthermore, exercise is important in maintaining the health of the immune system. Many diabetic athletes, such as the professional hockey player Bobby Clarke (more about him in Chapter 5), have shown that diabetes need not be a barrier even to strenuous sports. Indeed, there are a large number of diabetic marathon runners.

Currently, exciting efforts are under way to prevent type I diabetes. There is some hope that a breakthrough may be on the horizon. The next chapter, which covers the progress in treating autoimmune diseases, will discuss these efforts in more detail.

LUPUS

Systemic lupus erythematosus, commonly known simply as lupus, affects at least 500,000 Americans, according to one estimate. The numbers are not known with certainty because lupus is so difficult to diagnose. Experts believe that as many as half of those stricken with lupus may not even know they have the disease.

Lupus has been described in documents thousands of years old. The name *lupus* is a Latin word meaning "wolf." It may have been chosen originally because the skin condition that accompanies the disease eats away at the face with wolflike aggression. Or perhaps it was chosen because people with the disease resembled wolves or appeared to have been bitten by wolves. Whatever its source, the name has been used through the ages.

Lupus is an immune system malfunction in which the body's defenses turn on certain large molecules within the nuclei of body cells. Antibodies to these molecules can be found in virtually all victims of lupus. Because these autoantibodies spread throughout the body, the symptoms of lupus can affect many body components, including the blood, joints, nervous system, and kidneys and other organs.

The most obvious symptom is a rash, which usually spreads across the nose and cheeks in the shape of a butterfly. But the rash appears in less than a third of people with lupus. Most lupus patients suffer the aches, pains, and swollen joints that are typical of arthritis. Extreme fatigue is common among lupus

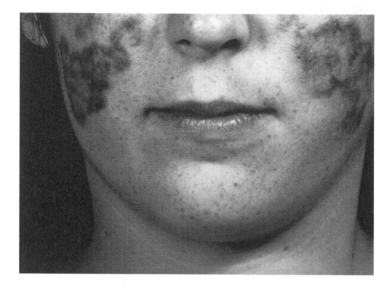

Lupus sometimes causes a rash
over the nose and cheeks.

victims. The disease can also cause mouth ulcers; fevers; anemia; weight loss; pale, numb fingers; discomfort in cold weather; skin rash after exposure to sun; and sensitivity to light.

Few lupus patients have all the symptoms and many of the symptoms they experience may be mild. Lupus patients may show no signs of the disease at all while it goes into remission for weeks, months, and even years. As in other autoimmune diseases, the symptoms may flare up without warning and disappear just as quickly, or they may last for a long time. This makes diagnosis difficult. The symptoms of lupus are often mistaken for indications of skin infection, rheumatoid arthritis, or kidney disease. Lupus patients commonly have the disease from three to ten years before it is diagnosed.

Once lupus is suspected, however, blood tests can usually easily detect the disease by checking for the autoantibodies that cause lupus. Blood tests are not foolproof, though, as some individuals who have these antibodies do not get the disease.

In most cases lupus is a disease that people live with rather than die of. The vast majority of patients have a normal life expectancy and experience mild to moderate symptoms. But about 10 percent of the cases are fatal, usually because of internal bleeding, lowered resistance to infection, and complications involving the kidneys and other internal organs.

Until recently, lupus was considered a dangerous condition for pregnant women. But today, with care and careful monitoring, most women with lupus can have healthy babies. That is a significant advance because lupus primarily strikes women of childbearing age. Indeed, only one out of ten lupus cases involves males.

For unknown reasons, three times more black women than white contract lupus. But it has been known to affect people of all races and ages. The most important risk factor identified with lupus is family history. At least six genes have been connected with the disease. The greater the incidence of lupus among relatives the greater the chances of contracting it. But, as with all autoimmune diseases, a mystery remains as to what triggers the disease. Viruses, drugs, pollutants, and sunlight are all suspected of setting the autoimmune system on a wrong course that results in lupus.

There is no cure for lupus. Most patients require medication of some kind to relieve pain and swelling. Aspirin is the most common drug prescribed. Powerful antiinflammatory and immunosuppressant drugs such as steroids are used in severe cases. Doctors are cautious about these medications because they can produce harmful side effects, including deterioration of joints, depression, weight gain, increased risk of infection, digestive problems, hair loss, and sterility.

Doctors recommend plenty of rest for lupus patients as well as a proper diet and regular exercise. Sunscreen is also prescribed to guard against any possible flare-ups connected with sunlight.

MULTIPLE SCLEROSIS

Multiple sclerosis, commonly referred to by its abbreviation MS, is another notoriously variable autoimmune disease. It is one of the most common diseases of the central nervous system in the United States, affecting between 250,000 and 350,000 individuals.

Multiple sclerosis occurs when the immune system attacks myelin, the protective covering surrounding nerves. Myelin sheaths act as insulators to contain the electrical impulses of the nerves. The brain controls muscles and sensory organs with these impulses. The term *multiple* is used because the disease often strikes at a number of randomly spaced sites along the central nervous system, which consists of the spinal cord and the brain. *Sclerosis* refers to the scarring that results from the loss of myelin at these sites.

The most common symptoms of MS are blurred vision, loss of balance, tremors, and slurred speech. Many people with multiple sclerosis complain of fatigue, rapid involuntary eye movement, and a weakness, tingling, or numbness in the limbs. As in many autoimmune diseases, the symptoms may come and go without any obvious pattern. Flare-ups, remissions, and relapses are common. The attacks usually occur most frequently three to four years after the disease first strikes. But Arney Rosenblat of the the National

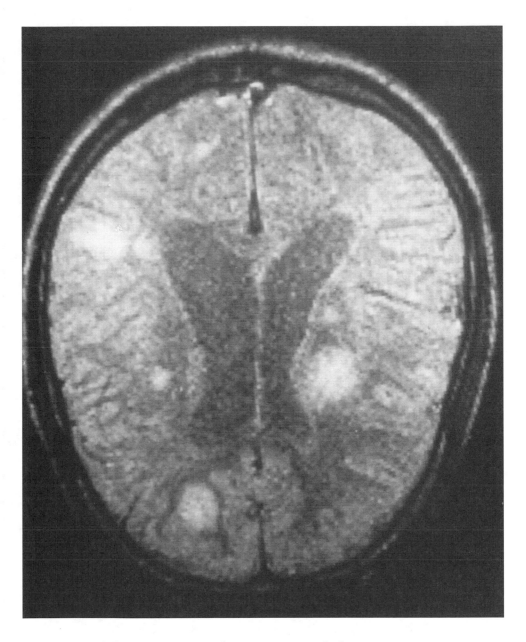

The white spots on this cross section of a brain are scars that result from multiple sclerosis.

Multiple Sclerosis Society cautions that "the multiple sclerosis experience is different for each individual."[3]

The disease does not kill, but it can disable. Roughly 20 percent of those with MS either use wheelchairs or are confined to bed. In some cases, mild fatigue is the only symptom. Most cases fall somewhere in between the two extremes in severity.

Multiple sclerosis is neither contagious nor inherited, although the risk of its developing is greater if a relative has the disease. As is typical of many autoimmune diseases, more women than men have multiple sclerosis. The ratio is about two to one. The disease most often strikes young people in their twenties and thirties. Some experts believe that susceptibility to the disease is acquired before the age of fifteen. Rarely does MS strike people before the age of fourteen or after fifty-five.

One of the curious aspects of multiple sclerosis is its relation to geography. The disease is most common among people with a Western European background and those who live in temperate climates. Americans living in the southern part of the United States get the disease in smaller numbers than those living in the northern regions. MS is relatively rare in Asian countries and has never been reported among certain African populations. This is especially baffling because African Americans are no less likely than white Americans to have the disease.

As with lupus, the tremendous variability of MS makes it difficult to diagnose, especially in the early stages. A diagnosis of multiple sclerosis is usually not made unless a person has had at least two attacks of MS symptoms stemming from different parts of the central nervous system. For example, the person might have had one attack of blurred vision and another in which there was a tingling or near-numbness

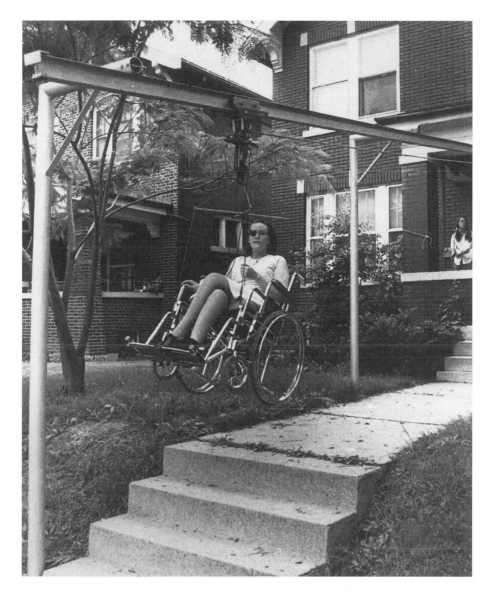

*Because she has a severe form of multiple sclerosis,
this young woman is unable to control her muscles and
must use a wheelchair. The mechanism on the
sliding track helps her maneuver the wheelchair.*

*Researchers are trying to figure out why multiple
sclerosis affects some populations more than others.
Certain African populations, for example,
never get multiple sclerosis.*

in the legs. Magnetic resonance imaging can reveal
the effects of MS by providing views of the structures
of the central nervous system.

Multiple sclerosis is often a progressive disease,
which means that the patient's condition gradually
worsens. In keeping with its unpredictability, though,
cases of complete recovery have been reported. The

mysterious nature of the disease leaves people with MS vulnerable to false claims and fad treatments, especially in the most severe cases.

Most accepted medical treatment is aimed at relieving uncomfortable symptoms and helping patients to retain as much muscle control as possible. Steroids can help them recover from serious attacks but have shown no long-term benefits in preventing the progression of the disease. Physical therapy helps patients to keep their muscles functioning as well as possible.

GRAVES' DISEASE

Graves' disease is named after the nineteenth century Irish physician Robert Graves, who first reported the disease. It is an autoimmune condition that affects the thyroid gland. However, the immune system does not attack and destroy the thyroid gland; rather the immune response stimulates the gland into excess hormone production.

The thyroid gland is located at the base of the throat. This gland secretes hormones that control the body's rates of growth and metabolism by regulating the rate at which it processes nutrients. A person who has too much thyroid gland activity is said to have a *hyperthyroid* condition; a person with too little has a *hypothyroid* condition. Graves' disease is the leading cause of hyperthyroidism.

Like many autoimmune diseases, Graves' disease most commonly occurs in people between the ages of twenty and forty. It is at least five times as likely to affect women as men.

Graves' disease is difficult to detect because the symptoms are not definite or distinctive. Those with the disease tend to be nervous, anxious, or irritable. They often have a fast heartbeat, tolerate heat poorly, and have trouble sitting still or resting. Sudden weight loss is common. The eyes often become puffy and watery and may even bulge as a result of pressure from swollen tissue behind the eyes. Graves' disease is not life-threatening and if treated usually causes no long-term difficulties other than lingering eye problems.

Once Graves' disease is suspected, it is easy to confirm with a blood test. Treatment is also relatively straightforward and effective. Antithyroid medication can reduce the amount of hormone produced by the gland. But about 5 percent of those treated this way experience allergic reactions to the medication.

As an alternative treatment, a single dose of radioactive iodine can usually destroy enough of the gland to cut hormone levels back to normal. Thyroid tissue can be surgically removed to achieve the same results. But both radioactive iodine and surgery run a risk of destroying too much of the gland and producing the sluggish symptoms of hypothyroidism. However, taking thyroid hormone supplements readily corrects the underactive thyroid condition.

AUTOIMMUNE HEMOLYTIC ANEMIA

Autoimmune hemolytic anemia is the sudden, relatively rare disease that attacked my son Evan (see Chapter 1). It occurs when the immune system attacks the body's red blood cells. The reason that happens is not known, although a virus is suspected of triggering the disease. Genetic factors may play a role, but the extent of that role has not been confirmed.

Normally, red blood cells survive about 120 days in the bloodstream, by which time they no longer perform their oxygen-carrying role efficiently. The spleen then removes the old red blood cells. In autoimmune hemolytic anemia, the immune system produces autoantibodies that attach themselves to the cell membranes of healthy red blood cells. It is not known whether the cells are directly destroyed by the immune system, or whether the spleen mistakenly identifies them as old cells or foreign debris. In either case they are removed from the blood. The vast numbers of red cells pulled out of the blood and into the urinary tract can produce a dark red urine.

This autoimmune reaction is often rapid and violent. In some cases, it may be life-threatening. Patients suffer from extreme fatigue and may have pale or jaundiced (yellowish) skin tones. Presence of the disease can be confirmed by a blood test.

A blood transfusion is the normal procedure when blood counts run dangerously low. But it may be difficult or impossible in the case of this disease because the transfused blood will likely be attacked as readily as the patient's own blood.

Autoimmune hemolytic anemia is not a long-term condition. Once the initial onslaught is weathered and the patient recovers, a recurrence is unlikely.

GUILLAIN-BARRÉ SYNDROME

The disease Guillain-Barré syndrome was named after two French neurologists who first reported the symptoms in World War I soldiers. Cases of Guillain-Barré syndrome are relatively rare: there is about 1 case per 100,000 people.

While the cause of the syndrome is unknown, it involves an antibody attack on nerves. The disease frequently strikes on the heels of another illness, often a virus. Apparently, Guillain-Barré can also be triggered by surgery, certain drugs, and bacterial infections. The symptoms usually appear between one week and one month after an illness or operation and increase in severity for about three weeks.

People with Guillain-Barré syndrome may experience weakness in all muscular areas of the body, muscle pain, and tingling in conjunction with near-numbness. These symptoms can be disabling but are usually short-lived. Patients can have serious complications, particularly when the muscles of the respiratory system are affected. Between 2 and 5 percent of people who have Guillain-Barré syndrome die. Of those who survive, 30 percent require a mechanical ventilator to assist their breathing. About 20 percent are left with some long-term disability, and the remaining 80 percent fully recover.

Physicians treat the condition by replacing the patient's blood with either *albumin* or *gamma globulin*, proteins found in blood. The treatment works presumably by eliminating the autoimmune antibodies from the body.

Guillain-Barré disease gained some notoriety in the United States in 1976. That year thousands of Americans contracted the disease within a few weeks of being inoculated for swine flu. Health authorities had requested a massive vaccination program for swine flu because of an alarming outbreak at the U.S. Army base at Fort Dix, New Jersey. The Fort Dix flu virus appeared similar to one that caused nearly half a million deaths in the United States in 1918. Medical authorities hoped to prevent a new catastrophic outbreak by vaccinating everyone.

But swine flu proved to be far less dangerous than medical experts had feared. In fact, the swine flu vaccination may have caused more harm than good. The incident generated great controversy over whether the vaccine had caused Guillain-Barré syndrome. Subsequent studies concluded that the vaccine did trigger an increase in cases of Guillain-Barré, but the increase was far less than originally reported.

ADDISON'S DISEASE

Addison's disease is a failure of the adrenal glands to produce natural steroids, such as *hydrocortisone*. The disease is usually caused by an autoimmune reaction. At one time, turberculosis, which can destroy the adrenal glands, was the major cause of this relatively rare disease. With the decline of tuberculosis in most industrial countries (until recently), autoimmune reaction has become the primary cause. In autoimmune-triggered Addison's disease, the body's immune system attacks and destroys the adrenal glands.

Symptoms of Addison's disease include low blood pressure, weakness, loss of appetite, sluggishness, weight loss, nausea, darkening of the skin, and abdominal pains. It is diagnosed by measuring the amount of steroids in blood and urine.

Adrenal failure is a potentially life-threatening condition. Presently, it is incurable, but if the disease is detected early, it is easily controlled. Doctors usually prescribe daily steroid tablets, primarily hydrocortisone, to replace the absent natural steroids. Acute cases may require injections of steroids and a salt solution.

With appropriate replacement of natural steroids, most people with Addison's disease can live a fully active life and require no special diets or precautions. John F. Kennedy, for example, did not let Addison's disease stop him from campaigning vigorously and performing the demanding duties of President of the United States.

PSORIASIS

Psoriasis is a skin disease that affects from 1 to 2 percent of the American population. Although it can strike at any age, it is most often first seen in teenagers and young adults. Psoriasis can be easily distinguished from other skin diseases by red scaly patches, ranging from teardroplike spots to giant plaques that cover the entire abdomen or back. The patches most often appear on the scalp, elbows, and knees, but they can occur any place and may cover from 20 to 80 percent of the body.

Psoriasis is a chronic disease: most patients have difficulty with it throughout their lifetime. Although it is rarely life-threatening, it can be emotionally upsetting and a source of continual discomfort. To hide their skin condition, many people with psoriasis never go to the beach and avoid all situations in which they would have to remove clothing in front of other people. In about 10 percent of cases, psoriasis is accompanied by a disfiguring form of arthritis.

Its cause is not completely understood, but it is known that skin cells called *keratinocytes* multiply seven times faster in the red patches than in normal skin. Psoriasis is suspected of being an autoimmune disease because T-cells seem to play a role in the abnormal cell growth and the inflammation that accompanies it. But whether the immune activity is the cause or effect of the cell growth is unclear.

Since psoriasis runs in families, it has been suggested that certain abnormal T-cells can be inherited.

It may be that these cells are never activated in some people, but in people with psoriasis, they could be triggered by any number of stresses, such as skin injury, bacterial infection, or emotional upset.

Psoriasis is incurable, but it can be controlled. Some people can clear their psoriasis patches simply by lying on the beach in the sun. However, this natural treatment carries with it the risk of skin cancer. For small patches, doctors recommend applying cortisone creams, tar-based creams, or a new cream that contains an ingredient related to vitamin D.

More severe cases are treated by exposing the skin to ultraviolet light. Drugs, such as cyclosporine and methotrexate, are prescribed only in extreme cases because they can have serious side effects. They work by inhibiting the activity of the immune system. No matter what treatment is chosen, it must be ongoing to prevent symptoms from reappearing.

Doctors are still a long way from unraveling the mystery of psoriasis. But the rapid strides made in the last few years have given dermatologists optimism that a safe and effective cure will someday be found.

4

CLOSING IN ON
AUTOIMMUNE
DISEASES

The medical world has made occasional break-throughs in the treatment of autoimmune diseases over the years. A good example is the discovery of insulin. But little progress has been made in preventing or curing these illnesses. Researchers have been thwarted by their inability to pinpoint the causes of autoimmune diseases and by the complex mysteries of the immune system. Without a clear idea of what targets to aim at, medical researchers have been unable to develop medical weapons to combat autoimmune diseases. Furthermore, research has been a low priority until recently because the medical community formerly believed that these diseases were not widespread. Another reason is that in most cases, autoimmune diseases are not life threatening.

But as more and more diseases have been linked with a faulty immune system response, this area has become a hot research topic. An effective autoimmune drug would most likely bring in billions of dollars in revenues. As a result, pharmaceutical companies have joined academic researchers in exploring possible cures and preventive treatments.

One promising approach to a treatment is immune suppression—the process of artificially turning off or slowing down the immune response. Steroids work this way, but in a shotgunlike manner. The steroids cortisone and *prednisone* have been the prime treatment for most autoimmune diseases in the past few decades. In order to turn off the particular immune reaction that causes the disease, steroids must attack the entire immune system. But when the immune system is weakened as a result, the body is vulnerable to anything that might invade it. Immunosuppressant drugs are so powerful that they cause many unwelcome and even dangerous side effects. Typically, they are useful only for a short time, and they do not provide any long-lasting benefits.

Recently researchers have achieved more promising results with a substance called *cyclosporine*. Cyclosporine targets only the T-helper cells, the T-cells that help speed up the production of antibodies. Thus, the drug suppresses these cells while leaving the rest of the immune system response intact.

Since cyclosporine first became available in 1984, it has shown an ability to prevent and cure several types of autoimmune diseases. The drug works particularly well against psoriasis. Tests have shown that cyclosporine can clear up psoriasis in 98 percent of cases. The drug has also been effective in reducing the swelling of arthritic joints, though it cannot undo the structural damage that rheumatoid arthritis inflicts on joints and ligaments.

Cyclosporine is far from a miracle cure. As one doctor says, the drug has shown "remarkable results, but there are still insufficiencies and problems."[1] There is some question of how long it can be safely used in treating disease. For example, prolonged use of cyclosporine has been connected with kidney damage. Nevertheless, cyclosporine has shown promise as a tool in fighting autoimmune diseases.

Researchers have been on the lookout for other immunosuppressant drugs that are even more effective and less toxic than cyclosporine. Recent experiments at the University of Pittsburgh have yielded encouraging results with a drug called FK 506. Nine psoriasis patients, four of whom also had rheumatoid arthritis, were given FK 506 in a carefully controlled trial. The drug completely cleared the psoriasis in all nine cases within three to four weeks. It also relieved many of the symptoms of rheumatoid arthritis in the four patients. The medication, however, did not provide a long-term cure. The diseases tended to reappear when the patients were taken off the drug. FK 506 also caused some minor, short-term side effects, such as headaches and nausea. The long-term side effects have not yet been studied.

The drug *azathioprine* has been commonly used to prevent immune system rejection of organ transplants. Researchers at the University of Florida have been probing the immune-suppressing qualities of this drug to see whether it could prove useful in treating autoimmune diseases.

The results of their tests have so far been encouraging. Azathioprine has shown the potential to prevent type I diabetes in some youths and may slow down or halt the progress of the disease in those who already have it. A seventeen-year-old type I diabetic boy taking part in the study has been free of daily insulin injections for almost three years. His treatment consisted of two pills a day for only two months. Azathioprine apparently halted the body's immune system attack on insulin-secreting cells of the pancreas and allowed them to recover so that they could continue producing insulin without the help of the drug. Long-term effects of this drug are not known, however.

Another promising new drug goes by the un-wieldly name of CTLA41g. This substance shuts off the immune response by interrupting the communications between T-cells and antigen-presenting cells. Researchers tested it by injecting laboratory mice with two foreign substances. As expected, the mice produced antibodies to each substance. The researchers then injected the mice with CTLA41g. The drug suppressed the production of both types of antibody.

In an experiment performed at the University of Chicago, scientists grafted insulin-producing pancreatic cells from a human into the kidneys of mice. Some of these mice were then treated with CTLA41g while others were not. The mice's immune systems normally would attack the foreign cells. The grafted cells in the treated mice survived for ninety days while those in the untreated mice lasted only six days. The treated mice also accepted further grafts from the same donor. No serious side effects were observed in any of the animals.

Several years of testing will be needed before the drug can even be tried in humans. It does not appear to be a permanent solution to autoimmune problems because the suppressing effect on the immune system does not last long. But the preliminary experiments indicate that CTLA41g may be a powerful weapon in fighting autoimmune disease. Not only does it work effectively, but it may be able to work selectively against a particular immune response rather than shutting down the whole works.

Medical researchers have been moving forward on another front in their search for a selective weapon that would not shut down the whole immune system.

It all began in 1911 with a man named H. Gideon Wells. He performed experiments with guinea pigs that had anaphylactic shock, the excessive immune reaction discussed in Chapter 2. He induced the reaction by injecting the guinea pigs with a foreign protein. Strangely enough, Wells found that he could prevent the anaphylactic shock if he fed the animals that same protein for several weeks before the injection. Wells was at a loss to explain the phenomenon.

This curious result put researchers onto a fascinating new pathway. They began trying to feed antigens to animals with autoimmune diseases. Multiple sclerosis, for example, has been cured in rats by feeding them the very substance that originally provoked the immune response. In MS, you may recall, the immune system attacks the myelin protein sheath surrounding nerves in the spine and brain. Researchers first induced an MS-like disease in rats by injecting the animals with a form of the myelin protein. When these same rats were later *fed* myelin protein, however, the rats were dramatically cured.

Taking the antigen in orally, thereby going directly to the stomach, seems to build the body's tolerance to the substance. Consequently, the treatment is known as *oral tolerization*. Although it is unclear how the cure works, there is speculation that the proteins may stop the T-cells from sending messages.

The early research on humans has shown great promise for treating multiple sclerosis, arthritis, and diabetes. Patients with multiple sclerosis took capsules containing a myelin protein; diabetes patients took insulin in a capsule; and people with arthritis ingested collagen in their orange juice. Many were able to reduce or completely eliminate the immune-suppressing drugs they were taking to control their disease.

If the research continues to hold up, doctors may be on to an extremely valuable disease-fighting tool. This method of immune suppression is very selective: it blocks only the immune response against the proteins that are ingested. Since any given antigen provokes a response from only a few T-cells in a million, the method leaves the overwhelming majority of the immune system intact. The method also produces no apparent side effects. Dr. Howard Weiner, an immunologist at the Brigham and Women's Hospital in Boston, says it is "so simple and apparently so safe that it seems too good to be true."[2]

The immune system's selective reaction to ingested proteins leads researchers to believe that they can create a vaccine that would work against T-cells. If autoimmune diseases are indeed caused by T-cells that misidentify antigens, immunologists may be able to thwart the diseases by fine-tuning a vaccine that protects the human body from its own renegade T-cells.

Currently experiments are under way to test the effectiveness of T-cell vaccines. A Dutch group has begun tests with rheumatoid arthritis patients. A Boston effort is under way to test a vaccine for multiple sclerosis. Although results of the tests will not be known for some time, early reports show that the vaccines have no immediate side effects.

A variation on this approach is to engineer antibodies that will attack only certain renegade T-cells. In one test, fifty patients with severe arthritic symptoms were given a single dose of antibodies to T-cells. Three-fourths of these patients experienced a dramatic reduction in pain and swelling. Similar results were obtained with antibodies given to a smaller group of multiple sclerosis patients. According to Hubert J. P. Schoemaker, who heads Centecor, Inc., a biotechnology company in Malvern, Penn., the technique could be "a major breakthrough if the effect continues to be found in large trials."[3]

Another high-tech approach in the fight against autoimmune diseases involves blocking immune cells with chemicals. One type of chemical blocking currently under study involves tying up the harmful T-cells with harmless molecules. Copies of the surface marker molecules that have stimulated the T-cell attack are injected into an inflamed joint. There they latch onto the T-cells and prevent them from attacking the body's cells.

Some researchers believe that it is not faulty T-cells but rather faulty MHC in the antigen-presenting cells that causes autoimmune diseases. If that is true, then scientists may find a cure for autoimmune diseases in genetic engineering. Perhaps new genes could be inserted to repair or reprogram the faulty MHC genes. This solution will become more of a reality when researchers achieve the ambitious goal of the Human Genome Project to isolate and catalogue the estimated 100,000 genes that direct a person's chemical makeup. This knowledge would also make it possible for scientists to zero in on precise genetic markers that indicate who is at risk for autoimmune disease. Physicians might then be able to stop the disease before it began.

One fortunate aspect of autoimmune diseases is that methods developed against one disease can probably be adapted to many other autoimmune diseases. The rapid rate at which scientists are closing in on the secrets of the immune system offer hope that major advances in fighting autoimmune diseases are just around the corner. However, because of the complexity of the immune system, most researchers doubt that the diseases will be cured in the near future.

5

LIVING WITH AUTOIMMUNE DISEASE

Until researchers make a significant breakthrough in curing autoimmune diseases, patients must learn to cope with them from day to day. Each case of autoimmune disease is unique in the way it affects a person's life. But much can be gleaned about these temperamental diseases from the individual stories of people who have them. The following case histories show how a few well-known people are dealing with their autoimmune conditions.

WHITE HOUSE MYSTERY

Barbara Bush was never one to crave attention. Yet George Bush's election in November of 1988 put her in the spotlight as America's First Lady. While she was trying to settle into her new White House home in early 1989, she began experiencing symptoms that would push her even further into the public spotlight.

First, she began losing weight. Although she was eating normally, she lost eighteen pounds in three months. Mrs. Bush paid no attention to this early warning. Later, she would scold herself for this, saying, "How can any grown-up in America be so dumb as to think weight would just fall off?"[1]

Eventually, when her eyes became swollen and irritated, she did seek medical help. Rumors spread that the sixty-four-year-old First Lady was going blind. Tabloid newspapers claimed that she was near death.

Barbara Bush's problem turned out to be much less serious. Doctors diagnosed her condition as Graves' disease. The First Lady had a simple explanation for what had happened: her thyroid, the gland responsible for regulating her metabolism, "just went wacko."[2]

Mrs. Bush was treated with a dose of radioactive iodine to slow down her overactive gland. It was not long before she returned to her normal daily activities, including her one-mile swim. Although the thyroid problem was relatively easy to treat, she continued to be bothered by puffy eyes and occasional double vision. In August 1989, several months after she was first treated for Graves' disease, her physicians gave her the steroid prednisone in the hopes of reducing the swelling in the tissues around her eyes. The drug had little effect, so they tried giving her a series of radiation treatments over ten days.

While Mrs. Bush was recovering, her husband was taking part in a high-stakes game of nerves over Iraq's invasion of Kuwait. The president formed an international coalition of armies to drive the Iraqi dictator Saddam Hussein out of Kuwait. In early 1991, the coalition forces won a spectacular military victory in the month-long Persian Gulf War.

But the pressure of the conflict seemed to take its toll on the president. He was restless, jittery, unable to sleep. By early spring George Bush was thirteen pounds below his normal weight.

The president took pride in his history of excellent health. During his eight years as Vice-President, he had not missed a single day of work because of illness. At a trim six feet two inches, 195 pounds, he regularly exhausted friends and observers with his active schedule. He managed to combine plenty of sports and recreation with his official duties. In March 1991 after a thorough physical exam, President Bush was declared to be in perfect health despite his slight weight loss. Two months later, the President trotted off on a late afternoon jog while staying at the presidential retreat at Camp David in Virginia. After running a short distance, he complained that he was not feeling well. He was unusually tired and short of breath, and his legs felt weak. His staff was particularly worried that his heartbeat had accelerated to a rapid, irregular pace.

Bush cut short the run and was flown to a hospital for tests. The doctors issued a stunning verdict. George Bush was suffering from Graves' disease—the same autoimmune disease that had struck his wife eighteen months earlier. Some experts estimated that the odds of a husband and wife both contracting the noncontagious disease was one in three million. In another bizarre twist, the Bushes' springer spaniel Millie was diagnosed as having lupus, an autoimmune disease rarely found in dogs.

For the first time, autoimmune diseases attracted national attention. Suddenly people were curious as to what caused these problems. Because the odds against George and Barbara's having the same illness were so enormous, investigators began searching for some environmental cause. Dan Quayle, who was then vice-president, began to feel uneasy living at the vice-presidential residence where the Bushes had spent the previous eight years. He wondered whether there was some contaminant, perhaps in the plumbing of the

Both George and Barbara Bush were diagnosed with Graves' disease when they were living in the White House as President and First Lady.

one-hundred-year-old mansion, that could be causing Graves' disease. Investigators began testing the water, not only at the vice-presidential residence but also at the White House, Camp David, and the Bushes' vacation home in Kennebunkport, Maine. They were looking for high levels of lithium, lead, and iodine.

The White House was deluged with telephone calls from concerned citizens offering advice and theories about the First Family's illness. A number of people suggested the Bushes start eating broccoli, the vegetable the president was known to despise. One caller urged the president to slather lemon juice over his throat and chest as a cure for his problems.

Autoimmune experts tried to calm the rampant rumors and misinformation about Graves' disease. They pointed out that the search for toxic elements in the water was probably a waste of time. An unlikely level of from ten to fifty times the normal intake of iodine was necessary to trigger a thyroid reaction. Another element under investigation, lithium, was known to decrease—not increase—thyroid activity in rare cases.

Instead, medical experts suggested that some hereditary factor probably made the Bushes vulnerable to the disease. Both Barbara and George had relatives with autoimmune diseases, though not Graves' disease. Some experts speculated that a virus passed from one Bush to the other could have triggered both autoimmune diseases. Others suggested that the stress of the presidential campaign, compounded by the Persian Gulf War, may have triggered them. Still others were unconvinced that stress played any important role in inducing autoimmune diseases.

Like his wife, the president was treated with radioactive iodine to suppress the overactive thyroid. Neither George nor Barbara was seriously affected by Graves' disease, although Barbara's eye symptoms lingered for many months. Fortunately, George's eye problems were not so troublesome. The two continued in the White House into 1993 as George made an energetic but unsuccessful bid for a second term in office.

Public awareness of autoimmune diseases increased a great deal as a result of the Bushes' development of Graves' disease while they were in the White House. However, despite a vigorous hunt for the source of the disease, much of the mystery remains.

AGAINST ALL ODDS

Rheumatoid arthritis is often thought of as a crippling disease. But the disease did not prevent the master artist Pierre-Auguste Renoir from continuing his work. At the age of fifty-six, he developed arthritis that severely damaged the joints of his hands and legs, and confined him to a wheelchair. Yet he managed to create some of his most beautiful paintings later in life.

Perhaps the ultimate example of a person who refuses to give in to the symptoms of rheumatoid arthritis is Lynn Adams. She has been called the Martina Navratilova of professional racquetball. Since the creation of the Women's Professional Racquetball Association in 1979, this six-time national champion has won more matches, honors, and money than any other player. And she has won every one of those matches while saddled with rheumatoid arthritis.

Lynn took after her parents, who were both excellent athletes. Her father, for example, had been offered a baseball contract by the Boston Red Sox. Sports was Lynn's main reason for living.

When she was sixteen, Lynn awoke one morning with throbbing wrist pain. Her wrist was so swollen and painful that she thought she must have broken it.

Her parents took her to the hospital emergency room, but X rays found nothing wrong. Three days later, the pain left almost as suddenly as it had come. Doctors speculated that the problem had been caused by an unknown virus.

But a week later Adams experienced the same type of pain and stiffness in her knee. Soon swelling and aches started popping up in other joints. Doctors examined her case further. Within a month of the appearance of her first symptoms, they diagnosed her illness as rheumatoid arthritis.

Adams was stunned. "I thought only old people got arthritis," she said.[3] Not until several years later did it sink in that this condition was going to stay with her the rest of her life.

An athletic career seemed out of the question. But Adams's doctor did not discourage her from remaining active in sports. While attending college, Adams developed a fierce style of racquetball. When the chance came to join the new professional racquetball tour, she jumped at it. She dropped out of college so that she could get a job to pay her tour expenses. Lynn's parents supported her in her decision both financially and emotionally.

Adams was determined that rheumatoid arthritis would not get in the way of her sports career. Just as she looked for anything that would give her an edge in competition, she learned all she could about rheumatoid arthritis so that she might get an edge in combating it. She did whatever she could to minimize its effects by following a recommended diet, getting plenty of rest, and avoiding smoking and drinking.

Despite her best efforts, she occasionally suffered severe flare-ups of pain. These frustrated and angered her. But she learned to stop feeling sorry for herself while competing in a tournament held in honor of the

Special Olympics. Adams lost the title match and went to the awards stand feeling irritable. But when she saw the cheerful expressions of special needs children much worse off than she was, she decided she had no right to feel sorry for herself.

Adams trained relentlessly at her sport. The work paid off when she won the national title in 1982. Ironically, the victory almost destroyed her racquetball career. After working so hard and achieving her goal, Adams recalls, " I just flew home and cried for a month."[4] She suffered a terrible letdown and struggled to find her winning form.

For a time, she gave up racquetball and switched to tennis. The change of pace seemed to relax her. When she returned to racquetball, she regained her old enthusiasm and beat number-one-ranked Heather McKay to capture another national title in 1983. Adams added more national titles in 1985, 1986, and 1987.

But after her 1987 triumph, Adams suffered another discouraging health setback. She lost all feeling in her hands and feet. She could not tell whether she was gripping the racquet or not, and she could not make the ball go where she was aiming it.

In December, Adams was told that she might never play again. For the next four months she stopped all activity. But that fierce competitive drive made her try again. She quickly found that she would have to adjust her training and her style of play to her new problems. She could not run or lift weights because of the tingling and near-numbing sensations these exercises produced. But she was able to play racquetball three times a week with no problem. To cut down on the amount of running she had to do, she changed her style of play from a hard-hitting power attack to a game of finesse. "That took a big mental

Lynn Adams overcame arthritis symptoms to win seven national racquetball championships. She won the last two when she had multiple sclerosis as well as arthritis.

adjustment," she says, "because I like to think of myself as a fast, macho player."[5]

In the early rounds of the 1988 championships, Adams struggled through her victories. But in the later rounds she surprised herself by playing some of the best racquetball of her life. In the finals, she easily defeated Caryn McKinney for her fourth straight national title. "I don't know where it came from," she said, commenting on her comeback.[6]

Adams went on to win another national title in 1990. The following year, doctors told her that the numbness and other symptoms that had begun four years earlier resulted from multiple sclerosis. Aside from putting her preceding accomplishments in an even more impressive light, the new diagnosis gave further evidence of the close relationship between autoimmune diseases.

Adams's advice for those learning to cope with rheumatoid arthritis is simple. "Find ways to work around it," she said.[7] Attitude is important. Adams says she always tries to remember that her handicap could be much worse than it is, and to feel lucky rather than unlucky.

Most of all, Adams, who frequently makes appearances on behalf of the National Arthritis Foundation, urges arthritis sufferers not to give in to the disease. "No one with arthritis should give up their favorite activities without a fight," she says.[8]

A HOCKEY SUPERSTAR

Like Lynn Adams, thirteen-year-old Robert Earle Clarke was not about to give up playing sports without a fight. The youngster from Flin Flon, Manitoba, Canada, had been diagnosed with type I diabetes after displaying all the classic symptoms—weight loss, constant thirst, and blurred vision. A simple blood test verified that his blood sugar level was too high. Doctors told Bobby that after a two-week stay in the hospital to get his blood sugar level back to normal, he would have to begin giving himself regular injections of insulin.

Many youngsters might recoil at suddenly learning they have to poke themselves with a needle every day, but Bobby took the news in stride. If he had to give himself insulin shots to stay well, that's what he would do. One thing he was not willing to sacrifice, however, was his athletic activities. At that time, the 1960s, many doctors advised diabetics to avoid strenuous sports, especially contact sports. Bobby was lucky. His doctor gave him the green light, as long as he promised to take care of himself.

That meant never skipping meals and avoiding eating sugar. His mother had to weigh all his food to make sure he was getting the right amount of each nutrient. Fortunately, his parents did not baby him. Bobby was allowed to leave home on camping trips as long as he packed his insulin.

No one knew why Bobby Clarke got the disease. The only case of diabetes in his family's medical history involved a great aunt who died of the disease before the turn of the century.

As Clarke advanced toward the highest levels of Canadian hockey, many people doubted that a diabetic could make it as a pro. But the disease got in Clarke's way only twice, and both times it was his carelessness about diet that caused the problem. The first occurred when Bobby was sixteen or seventeen years old and playing in a junior hockey league. His team was scheduled to play in a one o'clock game. Bobby suited up for the contest without eating lunch. After a while, as he puts it, "I started acting goofy, sort of like I was drunk."[9] Fortunately, a hospital was located across the street from the hockey rink. Bobby's coach walked him over and after treatment, Bobby quickly returned to normal.

The second incident occurred just after the Philadelphia Flyers ignored skeptics and selected Clarke in the league draft of unsigned players. The Flyers scheduled an early morning practice, and Bobby showed up on the rink without eating breakfast. After the practice, as he was riding in a car with teammates, Clarke passed out in the back seat. The teammates rushed the nineteen-year-old to the hospital, where doctors were able to get his system back in balance.

The Flyers' team doctor knew a great deal about diabetes. He warned Clarke that serious problems with his kidneys and eyes could develop if he did not take better care of himself. Clarke followed the advice.

The rookie proved doubters wrong by earning a spot on the Flyers' team. He scored fifteen goals and thirty-one assists that first year. But what really impressed both teammates and opponents was his relentless and inspirational style of play. The New York Islander star Bryan Trottier remembers Clarke as a player who "didn't give you anything. He only took away."[10] Clarke played with such courage that *Sports Illustrated* described him as a man "with the guts of 10-dozen burglars."[11] Although he was smaller than average for a pro hockey player, Clarke threw himself against opponents—poking, shoving, jabbing—and accepting solid hits in return without complaint.

The Flyers so admired Clarke's selfless team spirit that when he was twenty-three, they made him the youngest team captain in league history. Clarke was the driving force behind the Flyers' meteoric rise from a hapless expansion team to a championship contender. Philadelphia's general manager called him "the single most important thing that ever happened to the Flyer organization."[12] Philadelphia head coach Fred Shero labeled Clarke "the greatest leader I've ever seen."[13]

In 1974 the Flyers advanced to the Stanley Cup finals against the Boston Bruins. The Bruins won the first game of the series. Early in game two, the Bruins took a two-zero lead on their home ice, where they had not lost to the Flyers in more than six years. Just when things looked bleakest for the Flyers, Clarke almost single-handedly got them back into the series. He controlled the puck on face-offs and played tenacious defense against Boston's ace scorer, Phil Esposito. He scored his team's first goal, set up the tying goal with only a minute remaining in the game, and then scored the game winner in overtime. The tide of the series turned and the Flyers went on to win the first of two Stanley Cup titles.

Throughout his fifteen years with the Flyers, Clarke kept his diabetes under control. He watched his diet carefully. He exercised six or seven days a week all year long, lifting weights, running, and swimming. He kept tabs on his blood sugar level with a glucose meter. The glucose meter "added years to my career," according to Clarke.[14] Before he had the instrument, he could only wonder whenever he felt tired during a game or practice whether his blood sugar level was off or whether he was just fatigued. A wrong guess could be harmful. By measuring his blood sugar level with a glucose meter before he left home and again after the game, Bobby could be certain he was getting just the right amount of insulin—without guesswork.

Hockey player Bobby Clarke (right), shown here in 1974—the year he helped the Philadelphia Flyers win the Stanley Cup—has had diabetes since he was thirteen years old.

Clarke has lived with diabetes so long that he no longer even thinks about it. He laughs when he hears that people think he has some secret that allowed him to play a rough sport despite diabetes. He did nothing more, he says, than listen to his doctors and take care of himself. He advises diabetics to take the right attitude toward the disease. "Don't use it as a crutch," he says, urging diabetics to go after their goals. "You can do it if you want."[15]

As a three-time most valuable player of the league and member of the Hockey Hall of Fame, Bobby Clarke knows what he's talking about.

THE LUCKY MOUSEKETEER

Annette Funicello seemed to lead a charmed life. She was the daughter of an auto repair shop owner and a homemaker in Utica, New York. By chance when she was twelve years old, she danced in a ballet performance attended by Walt Disney. Impressed, the entertainment wizard asked her to audition for his television show, "The Mickey Mouse Club," which began airing in 1955. Annette not only won her mouse ears but became the show's most popular Mouseketeer.

She moved on to appear in feature films as she grew older. On the silver screen, her combination of talent, self-discipline, and sweet nature made her everyone's fantasy date. Annette Funicello was the picture of old-fashioned wholesome virtue. While starring in a series of popular "beach party" films, she refused to wear bikinis. "I wouldn't even wear them around my own pool," she said.[16] Her everyday life was as clean as her image. When she tried to write an autobiography, the publishers rejected it because it was not sensational enough.

Funicello kept a low profile for many years as she settled down to marriage and raising her three children. But even though her work was limited largely to peanut butter ads, she never lost her huge following of fans.

In 1987 movie producers persuaded Funicello, then in her forties, to revisit her youth by rejoining old cast members in another beach party movie. But while filming *Back to the Beach*, Funicello began experiencing what she called "the weirdest thing."[17] After sitting or lying in the sand for a scene, she had trouble getting to her feet. Even her costars commented on her wobbly state and needled her with jokes about her age.

Shortly after this, her eyesight grew worse. Funicello visited her eye doctor several times. The first two times he prescribed stronger lenses for her glasses. But when she returned a third time in six months with her vision still deteriorating, he knew something was wrong.

She visited a neurologist, who recommended she undergo a magnetic resonance imaging (MRI) test to see what the problem was. Her head was put inside a helmetlike contraption. She was strapped onto something that she described as a conveyor belt, and she was moved inside a metal tunnel. For forty-five minutes she heard strange pounding noises as the machine collected images of her nervous system. The tests showed the scarring and inflammation of multiple sclerosis.

Funicello's first reaction was relief that her problem was not a brain tumor. For the next couple of years she felt fine physically most of the time, and she decided not to tell anyone except her immediate family about her disease. She did not want to upset her fans, who thought of her as leading the perfect life. She admits, "I wondered if people would still like me" if they knew about the disease.[18]

To calm her own children's worries about the MS, she openly explained the nature of her problem to them. For example, if she felt a burning sensation in her feet while they were watching TV, she would tell the kids about the symptom.

Funicello had to deal with her own fears, as well as her family's. The unpredictability of the disease frightened her and she tried not to think about the possibility of being confined to a wheelchair. Once while eating dinner, her hands began shaking so much that she

Annette Funicello, a former Mouseketeer on television's "The Mickey Mouse Club," discovered she had multiple sclerosis in her forties.

could not hold a fork. On another occasion, she fell so ill with a burning fever that she could not walk to the bathroom. But the bad days were always followed by good days.

During a 1990 concert tour, Funicello was still able to dance, though she had spells of dizziness. But by 1991 she was no longer steady on her feet. She took to walking with a cane and leaning more heavily on her husband's arm. When questioned about this in public she would blame tendonitis caused by years of dancing.

As time went on the problem grew more difficult to hide. On one occasion, a friend of one of her children saw her stagger and wobble as she got up to leave her table at a restaurant. He told Funicello's son that she looked as if she were drunk. Rumors began to fly about her illness. Reporters bugged her and called relatives, trying to get a scoop.

On July 8, 1992, Annette Funicello decided to put an end to the coverup and announced to the world that she had multiple sclerosis. She quickly found that her fears of being abandoned by fans were unfounded. Thousands of encouraging cards and letters flowed in, as well as many suggestions from multiple sclerosis patients for home remedies. Funicello found it a great relief not to have to hide her disease any longer.

Annette has kept active marketing a new line of perfume, although she has had to cut down on her travel. She has tried a number of treatments to relieve the symptoms of her disease. She has used steroids, herbal medicines, vitamins—even acupuncture. So far, though, nothing has worked. Like many patients with autoimmune diseases, Annette has discovered that attitude is one of her most effective weapons. She knows that this unpredictable disease will give her good days and bad days. On a bad day, she tries to calm herself and to remember that if she can get through the discomfort of today, tomorrow will be better.

GLOSSARY

albumin—a protein found in blood and other substances, such as egg whites.

anaphylactic shock—a violent allergic reaction to a normally harmless—or only mildly harmful—substance, such as shellfish or bee venom. The immune response is so overblown that it can sometimes kill the victim in the process of fighting the substance.

anemia—a condition in which there are not enough red blood cells in the blood. Red blood cells are necessary to carry oxygen throughout the body. As a result of anemia, a person becomes weak and the skin turns pale.

antibody—a substance manufactured by the body to fight a specific invader. It is made up of protein molecules arranged in such a way that its surface matches that of the toxin. The antibody marks the invader for destruction by attaching itself to the enemy's surface in the same way a key fits into a lock.

antigen—any invader that causes the body to generate an antibody. Examples are bacteria, viruses, protozoans, and toxins.

antigen-presenting cell (APC)—a B-cell that breaks off a piece of a foreign material and displays it on its surface for inspection by T-cells. The T-cell then determines whether an immune response is called for.

antitoxin—a substance produced by the body to fight a specific toxin or disease agent.

arthritis—any of 100 conditions involving inflammation of the joints and surrounding tissues.

autoantibodies—antibodies that mark healthy "self" tissues as the enemy.

autoimmune—a condition in which the immune system attacks its own body's cells rather than harmful foreign substances. *Auto* means "self"; *autoimmune* refers to a self-attacking immune system.

azathioprine—an immune-suppressing drug used to treat rheumatoid arthritis and diabetes.

bacteria—one-celled organisms (classified as plants) that can cause infections.

B-cell, or *B-lymphocyte*—a type of lymphocyte that makes antibodies.

cartilage—the elastic skeletal tissue found in joints and other parts of the body. Cartilage forms the contact surfaces in the joints and also provides structure to parts of the body such as the nose.

collagen—a structural protein that makes up connective tissue and bone.

connective tissue—body tissue that binds and supports the bones in the joints. It makes up ligaments and tendons.

cortisone—a steroid produced by the outer layer of the adrenal gland. It is a major drug in the treatment of autoimmune diseases.

cross-reaction—the accidental marking of a substance as an enemy by an antibody. It happens when the surface markers on the substance are similar to those on the antigen the antibody was designed to target. This is one possible mechanism operating in autoimmune diseases; the surface markers of healthy body cells may be similar to certain antigens.

cyclosporine—a drug that suppresses the immune system. It is used to treat autoimmune diseases and to prevent the rejection of organ transplants.

deoxyribonucleic acid (DNA)—the material that genes are made of. It consists of two spiraling strands of four nucleic acids chained together in a specific sequence. The sequence acts as instructions, or code, for the manufacture of proteins by cells. Each set of three nucleic acids represents a "codon," which encodes for a particular amino acid in the protein chain.

enzyme—a protein that facilitates body processes by catalyzing a chemical reaction.

gamma globulin—a fraction of blood proteins that is rich in antibodies.

gene—a sequence of DNA that holds the recipe for making one protein. Located in the nuclei of cells, genes are translated by the cell into the sequence of amino acids necessary to create the particular protein.

genetic marker—a piece of gene—a sequence of DNA—that appears at a specific site in the genome and that may help code for a particular physical characteristic. Genetic markers may be used to identify people who are susceptible to specific diseases.

glucose—a simple sugar that is produced by the breakdown of carbohydrates in the digestive process. If the level of glucose in the blood becomes too high, diabetes develops.

hemolytic—a condition in which red blood cells are destroyed. *Hemo* means "blood" and *lytic* means "decomposition."

hormones—proteins that stimulate cells to perform specific activities.

hydrocortisone—a steroid produced by the outer layer of the adrenal glands. Also called cortisol, it is a derivative of cortisone.

hyperthyroidism—a condition in which the thyroid produces too much hormone.

hypothyroidism—a condition in which the thyroid does not produce enough hormone.

immune system—the portion of the body, including white blood cells, lymph nodes, thymus, and spleen, that protects against germs and other disease organisms.

inflammation—a painful response to injury or attack in which body tissues redden, heat up, and swell in an attempt to keep out harmful agents.

insulin—a hormone secreted by the pancreas to help in digestion of carbohydrates. It makes it possible for glucose in the blood to enter body cells and provide energy for the cells. The lack of this hormone is responsible for diabetes.

lymph channels—a network of passageways through which lymphocytes travel to patrol the body for invaders.

lymph nodes—lumps of lymph tissue distributed along the lymph channels. B-cells manufacture antibodies here and T-cells reproduce here.

lymphocytes—a class of white blood cells that make up lymph tissue and move throughout the body in the blood and lymph channels. Various kinds of lymphocytes, including B-cells and T-cells, are the major agents of the immune system.

magnetic resonance imaging (MRI)—a powerful medical diagnostic technique in which magnetic fields are applied to the patient inside a large machine to get images of the inside of the body. MRI is especially useful for viewing soft tissues like the brain.

major histocompatibility complex (MHC)—the genes that contain the code for identifying self molecules versus foreign molecules.

pancreas—a gland located behind the stomach. It secretes digestive enzymes, including insulin.

phagocytes—white blood cells that eat foreign organisms.

prednisone—a steroid produced by the outer layer of the adrenal glands. It is used in one of the main treatments currently available for autoimmune diseases.

proteins—chains of various amino acids that fold into unique shapes. Each protein is manufactured inside a cell according to instructions given by a specific gene within the nucleus of the cell. Enzymes, hormones, and body structures are made of proteins.

protozoans—microscopic one-celled organisms, classified as the earliest animals, that can cause diseases.

red blood cells—the cells that carry oxygen through the blood to body tissues. They make blood red in color.

remission—a state, often temporary, in which the symptoms of an illness have spontaneously disappeared.

rheumatism—any condition involving the inflammation of bone and surrounding tissue. When it affects the joints, as it usually does, it is called arthritis.

rheumatoid arthritis—one of the more common forms of arthritis, affecting primarily the small joints of the hands and feet. It is an autoimmune disease.

spleen—an organ in the abdomen that destroys aging red blood cells, filters blood, and produces lymphocytes.

steroid—one of many potent hormones produced in the body. The corticosteroids, including cortisone, are derived from hormones produced by the outer layer of the adrenal gland. They have been important in treating autoimmune diseases.

superantigens—antigens that fit into many different receptors for surface markers. Because they act in much the same way as master keys, they may unleash the kind of broad, all-out immune attack that is seen in autoimmune diseases.

surface markers—molecules on the surface of cells and other microscopic entities. The molecules identify, or "mark," the entities. By trying to fit their surface markers into the shape of these markers, cells can seek out particular antigens or cell types.

T-cells—lymphocytes that patrol the body for invaders. When they find one, they signal the immune system to attack them. These cells are named for the thymus gland, where they are manufactured.

T-helper cell—a kind of T-cell that speeds up the B-cells' production of antibodies.

thymus—a small gland on the neck. It directs the development of T-cells.

thyroid—a gland at the base of the neck. It produces hormones that regulate the processing of nutrients. Thus, the thyroid controls the rates of growth and metabolism of the body.

tuberculosis—a communicable disease in which bacteria infect the lungs.

type I diabetes—the more severe, less common form of diabetes that usually strikes in adolescence. Treatment usually involves regular insulin injections. It is sometimes called juvenile or insulin-dependent diabetes.

type II diabetes—a disease that accounts for 95 percent of all cases of diabetes. It usually strikes after age forty and in most cases can be treated with dietary changes and exercise, rather than insulin injections.

virus—a submicroscopic entity that has no cells—only DNA and RNA enclosed in protein. Viruses have some characteristics of living things and some characteristics of nonliving things. The only way they can reproduce is by infecting living cells and commandeering their replication systems.

white blood cells—colorless cells in the blood that work as part of the immune system to protect the body against infection and disease.

SOURCE NOTES

Chapter 2

1. Mark Caldwell, "The Immune Challenge," *Discover*, December 1991, p. 59.

Chapter 3

1. Fred G. Kantrowitz, *Taking Control of Arthritis* (New York: HarperCollins, 1990), p. 2.
2. Joan O. Hamilton, "New Weapons to Defend the Body Against Itself," *Business Week*, December 3, 1990, p. 167.
3. Holly Miller, "Annette Fights Back," *Saturday Evening Post*, November 1992, p. 40.

Chapter 4

1. Pat Phillips, "Cyclosporine Hits Autoimmune Ills," *Medical World News*, September 1991, p. 56.
2. Jane E. Brody, "'Hair of Dog' Tried as Cure for Autoimmune Disease," *New York Times*, October 18, 1994.
3. Gene Bylinsky, "The New Attack on Killer Diseases," *Fortune*, April 22, 1991, p. 181.

Chapter 5

1. "People Making News," *U.S. News & World Report*, April 10, 1989, p. 17.
2. Giovanna Breu, "A Specialist Examines the Obscure Disease That Gives Eye Trouble to Thousands

and to Barbara Bush," *People Weekly*, January 29, 1992, p. 33.

3. Kantrowitz, p. 6.

4. Mariah Burton Nelson, "Lynn Adams: Beating the Odds to Be No. 1," *Women's Sports*, October 1985, p. 14.

5. "A Case of Never," *Women's Sports*, October 1988, p. 60.

6. *Ibid.*

7. Nelson, p. 13.

8. *Ibid.*

9. Bob Clarke, "A Veteran Hockey Player Takes His Shots to Control His Diabetes," *People Weekly*, March 28, 1983, p. 71.

10. Laurie Miffin, "Clarke: A Night to Remember," New York Times Biographical Service, November 1984, p. 1443.

11. Mark Mulvoy, "Jubilation and a Cup in Philly," *Sports Illustrated*, May 21, 1974, p. 34.

12. Miffin, p. 1443.

13. *Ibid.*

14. Clarke, p. 71.

15. *Ibid.*, p. 72.

16. Nancy Matsumoto, "Hope in Her Heart," *People Weekly*, August 17, 1992, p. 74.

17. *Ibid.*, p. 76.

18. Miller, p. 40.

BIBLIOGRAPHY

Abelson, Reed. "The Autoimmune Gold Rush." *Forbes* November 25, 1991.

Black, Pamela. "Turning off Renegade T-Cells." *Business Week* November 18, 1991.

Blacks, Amory. "The High Toll of Lupus." *Washington Post Health* November 19, 1991.

Breu, Giovanna. "A Specialist Examines the Obscure Disease That Gives Eye Trouble to Thousands and to Barbara Bush." *People Weekly* January 29, 1992.

Brown, Norman. "New Hope, Better Treatment for Arthritis Sufferers." *Better Homes & Gardens* April 1992.

"Bush's Heart Scare." *Newsweek* June 20, 1991.

Bylinsky, Gene. "The New Attack on Killer Diseases." *Fortune* April 22, 1991.

Caldwell, Mark. "The Immune Challenge." *Discover* December 1991.

Cantor, Robert. *Diabetes & Exercise.* New York: E. P. Dutton, 1982.

Clarke, Bob. "A Veteran Hockey Player Takes His Shots to Control His Diabetes." *People Weekly* March 28, 1983.

Cohen, Jon. "Mounting a Targeted Strike on Unwanted Immune Response." *Science* August 7, 1992.

Collins, Clare. "Diabetes—the Hidden Symptoms." *Redbook* April 1989.

Cowan, R. "Diabetes Marker Plugged as Brain Enzyme." *Science News* September 15, 1990.

Gorman, Christine. "Stalking Who Done It at the White House." *Time* June 10, 1991.

Grim, David R. "Guillain-Barré Syndrome." *Postgraduate Medicine* October 1991.

Hales, Dianne. "The Disease That Fools the Doctors." *Good Housekeeping* April 1992.

Hanson, Betty. "Raging Hormones in the White House." *Discover* January 1992.

Health & Medical Horizons. New York: Macmillan, 1990.

Horton, Richard. "Autoimmune—Towards the Year 2001." *Lancet* April 11, 1992.

Kantrowitz, Fred G. *Taking Control of Arthritis.* New York: HarperCollins, 1990.

Larson, David E., ed. *Mayo Clinic Family Health Book.* New York: William Morrow, 1990.

Marx, Jean. "Taming Rogue Immune Reactions." *Science* July 20, 1990.

Marx, Jean. "Testing of Autoimmune Therapy Begins." *Science* April 5, 1991.

Matsumoto, Nancy. "Hope in Her Heart." *Women's Sports* October 1985.

Miffin, Laurie. "Clarke: A Night to Remember." New York Times Biographical Service, November 1984.

Miller, Holly G. "Annette Fights Back." *Saturday Evening Post* November 1992.

Nourse, Alan E. *Your Immune System.* New York: Franklin Watts, 1989.

Phillips, Pat. "Cyclosporine Hits Autoimmune Ills." *Medical World News* September 1991.

Potts, Eve, and Marion Mork. *Understanding Your Immune System.* New York: Avon, 1986.

"Psoriasis: Still Breaking Hearts." *USA Today* October 13, 1989.

Rennie, John. "First Class Culprit." *Scientific American* April 1992.

———. "Formula for Diabetes?" *Scientific American* October 1992.

Sinha, Animesh, et al. "Autoimmune Diseases: The Failure of Self-Tolerance." *Science* June 15, 1990.

Tabbara, Imad. "Hemolytic Anemias: Diagnosis and Management." *The Medical Clinics of North America* May 1992.

Wagner, Richard. *New Complete Medicine & Health Encyclopedia*, vol. 2. Chicago: J. G. Fergusson, 1990.

INDEX

Page numbers in *italics* indicate illustrations

Bush, George, 79–84, *83*

Cancer, 27
Cell blocking, 76
Center for Neurological
    Diseases, 75
Central nervous system,
    58, 60, 62, 94
Clarke, Bobby, 54, 88–93,
    92
Cortisone, 45, 46, 72
Cortisone cream, 69
Cross-reactivity, 30
CTLA41g, 74
Cyclosporine, 69, 72, 73

Deoxyribonucleic acid
    (DNA), 34, 49
Dermatology, 69
Diabetes, 12, 46, 47, 48,
    49, *51. See also*
    Type I diabetes
Diphtheria, 16
Dobson, Matthew, 47

Faustman, Diane, 33
FK 506, 73
Flu virus, 27, 66
Food and Drug
    Administration, 37
Food poisoning, 35
Funicello, Annette,
    93–96, *96*

Gamma globulin protein,
    66

Genes, 33, 77
    DR4, 42
Genetics, 33–34, 38, 42,
    49, 64, 77
Genetic markers, 33, 49,
    51, 52, 77
Glucose, 48, 49, 54
Glucose meter, 91
Graves, Robert, 63
Graves' disease, 36,
    63–64, 80–84, *83*
Guillain-Barré syndrome,
    36, 65–67

Hazo, Gian Franco
    Bottazo, 37
Human Genome Project,
    77
Hydrocortisone, 67
Hyperthyroidism, 63
Hypothyroidism, 63, 64

Immune suppression, 72
Immune system, 10, 11,
    12, 15–38, *17, 19, 22,*
    25, 29, 32, 40, 47, 49,
    52, 58, 63, 64, 67, 71,
    72, 73, 74, 75, 76, 77
Immunology, 15, 31, 35, 76
Immunosuppressant
    drugs, 57, 73
Insulin, 47, 49, *51,* 52,
    54, 71, 73, 74, 89, 91
Insulin-dependent
    diabetes. *See* Type I
    diabetes

Iodine, 83

Julius Caesar, 39
Juvenile diabetes.
   See Type I diabetes

Kappler, John, 31, *32*, 36
Kennedy, John F., 67
Keratinocytes, 68
Koch, Robert, 15

Lead, 83
Lithium, 37, 83
Lupus, 55–58, 60
Lymphatic channels, *22*,
   24
Lymph nodes, *22*, 24

Magnetic resonance
   imaging (MRI), 44, 62,
   94
Major histocompatibility
   complex (MHC) gene,
   51, 77
Major histocompatibility
   complex (MHC)
   protein, *25*, 33, 51
Marrack, Phillipa, 31, 32,
   32, 35, 36
Metchnikoff, Elie, 16
Methotrexate, 45, 69
Minkowski, Oskar, 48
Multiple sclerosis, 12,
   58–63, *59*, *61*, *62*, 75,
   87, 88
      vaccine, 76

Myelin, 58, 75

National Arthritis
   Foundation, 88
National Institutes of
   Health (NIH), 52, 53,
   54
National Multiple
   Sclerosis Society, 60

Pancreas, 47, 48, 49, 52,
   73
Pasteur, Louis, 15
Phagocytes, 16, 18, 21,
   24
Prednisone, 72, 80
Protozoans, 15, 18
Psoriasis, 68–69, 72, 73

Radioactive iodine, 64,
   80, 83
Renoir, Pierre-Auguste,
   84
Rheumatoid arthritis, 12,
   33, 34, 37, 39–46, 56,
   72, 73, 75, 84–88, *87*
      vaccine, 76
Rosenblat, Arney, 60

Silicone, 37
Skin cancer, 69
Skin nodules, 43
Special Olympics, 86
Staphylococci, 35
Steroids, 58, 63, 67, 72,
   80, 96

Superantigens, 35, 38
Surface markers, 18, 19,
  23, 24, 30, 33, 76
Surface receptors, 27
Swine flu, 66
Systemic lupus
  erythematosus, 33.
  See also Lupus

T-cells, 18, 19, 21, *22*, 23,
  30, 31, 32, 35, 51, 52,
  68, 72, 74, 75, 76, 77
    killer, 24, *25*
Tetanus, *19*
Tobacco, 38
Toxins, 16, 18, 38
Thymus gland, 18, *22*,
  31, *32*
Thyroid gland, 36, 37,
  63, 64, 80, 83
Transplant procedures,
  28–30, 73
Trichloroethylene
  (TCE), 36

Tuberculosis, 67
Type I diabetes, 34,
  46–55, 73, 89–93
Type II diabetes, 47

Vaccines, 30, 66, 67, 76
Viruses, 15, 18, 26, 34,
  35, 36, 38, 57, 64
von Behring, Emil, 16,
  19
von Mering, Joseph, 48

Weiner, Howard, 76
Weiner, Steven, 37
Wells, H. Gideon, 74–75
White blood cells, *17*, 18,
  23

X rays, 43, *44*

Yersinia enterocolitica,
  36

Zinkernagle, R. M., 35